ALAN BERKEY

BEYOND EXPERTISE

HOW TRUST, VISION, *and* **DELIVERY**

WILL REDEFINE YOUR RELATIONSHIPS

with CUSTOMERS *and* COLLEAGUES

RIVER GROVE
BOOKS

Published by River Grove Books
Austin, TX
www.rivergrovebooks.com

Distributed by River Grove Books

Design and composition by Greenleaf Book Group and Teresa Muñiz
Cover design by Greenleaf Book Group and Teresa Muñiz

Publisher's Cataloging-in-Publication data is available.

Print ISBN: 978-1-63299-421-9

eBook ISBN: 978-1-63299-422-6

First Edition

Subject matter experts
are the most valuable
members of any organization.
Companies cannot prosper
without them—period.

CONTENTS

PART THREE: CHALLENGES

PART FOUR: BECOMING AN EXPERT

CONTENTS

PART FIVE: ESTABLISH TRUST

PART SIX: DETERMINE MUTUAL VISION

CONTENTS

PART SEVEN: ENSURE DELIVERY

INTRODUCTION

1

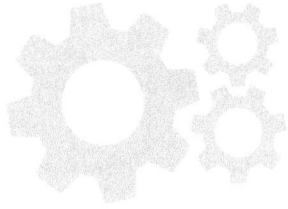

THE BEGINNING

Many years ago, I attended a high-level executive briefing at Ford Motor Company headquarters in Dearborn, Michigan. Ford had a strategic project underway to move all supplier-facing communications from fax, paper, and phone to the web. The initiative would impact the entire supply chain of more than 100,000 companies. As you can imagine, Ford's corporate leadership was extremely interested in the project.

Since I was intimately involved, the division director, Teri Takai (who would later become the chief information officer for the US Department of Defense), asked me to attend. At that time in my career, it was unusual to get that kind of executive-level visibility. I was young, new to the company, and inexperienced. Nevertheless, Teri requested my presence and I was happy to oblige.

Teri was allocated five minutes on the crowded agenda, and she asked me to present our progress and attempt to answer any questions. "But be prepared to be cut short," she warned, "or be skipped altogether if the meeting takes an unexpected turn."

Despite my junior status, I felt prepared. I knew the teams, the technologies, the schedules, the budgets, and the risks. I knew dozens of financial justifications for the massive investment the company was making. I knew what issues had been resolved and what barriers still lay ahead. I was confident I could answer any question.

Initially, the executives were patient with me. However, they quickly realized that my focus was too narrow for their needs and they started firing questions at me. Questions I could not answer. "How long will it take to replicate the technology and processes in Japan?" they asked. "Which key suppliers will be resistant?" they added. "We are facing a patent battle in Germany. How will this project complicate that case?" And on and on.

The five-minute presentation stretched past thirty minutes. Fortunately, Teri rescued me multiple times. She helped answer many of the questions, calm executive concerns, and gracefully deflect irrelevant issues. She focused the executives on the most urgent matters and created a feeling of excitement and optimism.

When the meeting ended, it was clear to all in attendance that Teri was the expert, not me. I was blindsided and flustered. Yet, how could that be? I knew more about this project than anyone in the company, including Teri, yet she came across as credible and trustworthy, not me. I wanted to know: What was I missing? How had I failed?

After that experience I began studying subject matter experts (SMEs) and taking notes. What do great experts do? How do some SMEs quickly establish trusting relationships? Why do people heed some experts but ignore others? What should I emulate and what should I ignore?

This book is the result of my decades of study and observations of SMEs. I believe SMEs are the most valuable members of any organization—period. They create vision, forge paths, create products, solve problems, sell customers, create policies, and cure ailments. Companies cannot prosper without them, and unlike non-experts, they provide the scaffolding upon which all other functions of the organization depend.

SMEs often hold top positions in their organizations. The chief executive officer of a start-up company is a subject matter expert. The chief technology officer of a multinational corporation is a subject matter expert. The head surgeon at an orthopedic practice is also a subject matter expert. But SMEs are not just the high-ranking professionals; they are often engineers, technicians, controllers, marketers, attorneys, doctors, therapists, and more. They hold the jewels of knowledge in their organizations and are typically the top performers in their fields.

Sometimes SMEs are assigned complimentary or flamboyant titles like "Sales Engineer," "Consultant," or even "Evangelist." But, more often, they are indistinguishable by title, rank, class, or pay scale.

Collectively, SMEs define the very pinnacle of organizational capability. They determine what can and cannot be done by their companies. SMEs also determine the economic prosperity and growth of their nations. They are the ones who get stuff done—if it can be done—and the ones who push the boundaries of accomplishment and creation.

Despite their universal value, few organizations fully appreciate the impact of these important people, nor do they establish procedures to magnify their influence. Instead, organizations often do not even know who their SMEs are, much less know how to help them. Even when organizations do acknowledge that key employees make disproportionately high contributions, they leave their effectiveness to chance.

Most executives genuinely believe that employees are their company's most valuable resources, yet few leaders take steps to develop SMEs comprehensively. Companies spend valuable time and money training employees on everything except the way to develop expertise and expert performance. They teach their employees about policies and technologies, for example, but they fail to fully develop their SMEs as experts. They fail to develop people in the very roles where they can make the greatest impact.

Effective SMEs are urgently needed in all industries and disciplines. Today's products are growing in sophistication, and markets are becoming increasingly complicated. Customers have become fickle, with increasing expectations and decreasing patience. Customer acquisition costs are high. Barriers to competitive entry are low. The global regulatory environments are fluid and onerous. Information, both true and false, abounds. At no time have effective SMEs been more necessary.

Ironically, although there is an urgent need for robust SMEs, public sentiment is shifting away from the wisdom of the experts. Technologies are encroaching on every expert domain. Global boundaries are opening to specialized competitors. Fakers are everywhere. SMEs now operate in a "post-truth" era where facts are depreciating in value and emotional sensitivities are amplified. The climate for SMEs is daunting.

After my decades of observation and study, I have identified many of the key ingredients that make a great SME. I wish someone had given me this book years ago, before I floundered trying to learn how to apply expertise in effective ways. It might have pointed me in a better direction, answered some of my questions, and spared my colleagues hundreds of hours of frustration.

This book is about the craft of the expert, or the artful application of expertise. It is about bringing your expertise out of the dark and maximizing your impact. It is about honing your influence with clients and boosting your authority with colleagues. In short, it is about becoming a compelling agent of change in any environment and with any audience.

In this book, I explore the techniques of the top experts. I examine what they do, and just as importantly, what they don't do to apply their expertise.

ESSENTIALS

2

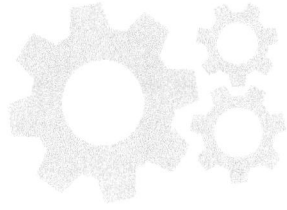

THE THINGS THAT MATTER MOST: TRUST, VISION, AND DELIVERY

Organizations depend on subject matter experts for broad and diverse purposes. Typically, SMEs are the keepers of collective corporate knowledge and the visionaries of product potential. Sometimes, they serve as company spokespersons or litigators. SMEs are routinely expected to identify the sources of vexing problems, implement solutions to those problems, and mitigate damages. They are expected to know things other people do not know, and they are expected to do things other people cannot do. Whether they are in engineering, law, medicine, finance, or some other field, SMEs must either know things well or be able to do things well (or most commonly, both at once). Even when knowledge and competence are established, however, an SME's purpose is not accomplished. To the contrary, knowledge and competence are just the beginning of an SME's job, not the end. Once knowledge and competence are firmly in hand, an SME can begin to deliver what is most needed: trust, vision, and delivery.

Establish Trust. SMEs must be masters at building and maintaining trust. No one in a corporation is better positioned than an SME to establish trust, and no one should be more capable of obtaining it. Top SMEs trust themselves and others. They don't display fear or discouragement. They are calm and confident.

Determine Mutual Vision. SMEs see and share a vision for the future. They recognize opportunities quickly and craft compelling solutions. They articulate the beginning, the end, and the path that connects the two. All great SMEs have vision, and they plant that vision in the hearts and minds of their audience.

Ensure Delivery. Experienced SMEs deliver desired results with a grace and consistency that others cannot match. Repeatable, flawless execution is the valuable feature that distinguishes great SMEs from average professionals.

The rest of this book is built around these three important objectives. Of course, other things are important to SMEs, but these three things matter most. If I worked with or managed SMEs in any capacity, I would remind them frequently of the importance of establishing trust, determining mutual vision, and ensuring delivery. For SMEs, everything fits within one of these three categories, or it must be relegated to second place.

3

DEFINING EXPERT

Before we jump into the details of trust, vision, and delivery, let's cover a few essential concepts about SMEs. The ideas and definitions needed for discussing our subject are not all self-evident.

A dictionary will tell you that an expert is someone who has more than average knowledge of a subject, or someone who can provide superior results. What the dictionary does not tell you, however, is that people often disagree about who is an expert and who is not. The word is vague, to be sure. There is no single diploma or degree, no standardized test, no clearly defined finish line that says you're an expert.

In some domains, it is easy to identify the experts. Objective criteria allow observers to measure degrees of proficiency. A chess master, for example, can consistently beat those who have less skill. Professional golfers and tennis players can outperform challengers. Medical specialists are more likely than junior practitioners to diagnose a disease correctly.

In other domains, identifying an expert is a highly subjective process and almost impossible to measure. Experts on foreign policy, law, accounting, finance, and many other fields will provide differing and often contradictory definitions. Wall Street is filled with experts who attempt to pick high-performing stocks, yet they fail nearly as often as they succeed. When objective criteria are not available, a person becomes broadly accepted as an expert when a sufficiently large number of people grant the title or when the person has practiced or studied in a field for a sufficient period of time.

Some people, of course, are universally recognized experts. The late Clyde Tombaugh is the astronomer who discovered Pluto. Jonas Salk invented the polio vaccine. Stephanie Kwolek invented bulletproof Kevlar. Muhammad Ali was an expert fighter, and Whitney Houston an expert singer. Few people would dispute that they were experts in their fields.

Unlike such superstars, however, most experts are not renowned. Most quietly serve their companies, customers, communities, and families. They don't seek public notoriety, yet they are experts in the truest sense. They are no less important and no less valuable to their constituents.

Herein is one of the most powerful qualities of an expert: You are not an expert because you think you are; you are an expert because someone else thinks you are. And when just one person thinks you are an expert, it means you are, to that person, an expert.

But being an expert in the eyes of one person does not make you an expert in the eyes of many, and being an expert in the eyes of many does not make you an expert in the eyes of all. You must earn the distinction repeatedly, with every person you meet, with every interaction.

The title of "expert" is a subjective concept; it is a belief that the expert is a source of superior performance or knowledge. It is the idea that you have power and value, that you are different, that your recommendations are worthy of consideration, that your opinion counts. Being an expert to the right person, the one person who needs you, can be more important and more life-changing than being an expert to many people.

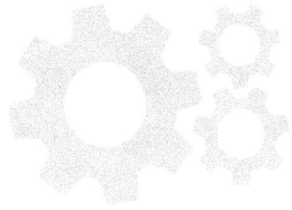

4

EXPERTISE

E xperts have been the subjects of curiosity and scrutiny for centuries. As stated in the previous chapter, they are often remarkable people who accomplish extraordinary things. Yet many experts are, in most respects, ordinary people with the same flaws and frailties as the rest of us. The experts, it can be easily pointed out, put their pants on one leg at a time.

It is precisely because experts have failings that this word can be so ambiguous, fleeting, and at times meaningless. Fortunately, researchers who study this subject work diligently to provide precise definitions and repeatable metrics of measurement. They try to bring objectivity to a subject where subjectivity is the norm. As the peer-reviewed literature states, an expert is someone who possesses an expertise, and that expertise encompasses the knowledge, skill, and attitude that distinguish that person from novices.[1]

Too many experts think that their impact will be determined by their level of proficiency in their field. They equate their expert status with their degree of know-how or technical skill. "I am an expert," they think, "because I am good at what I do." I am more knowledgeable than others. I am better educated, have more degrees, or put in more years of study. I have credentials. I deliver better results than others. These are some important aspects of being an expert, but they are not the whole package.

For experts to maximize their impact, they must be more than sages of knowledge or purveyors of facts. Experts who wield influence, who make a difference, who produce meaningful change, are those who surpass others in all three dimensions of expertise: knowledge, skill, and attitude.

Unfortunately, many experts see themselves in just one dimension. They achieve success in one way and cling to that dimension thereafter. Some experts even dismiss other dimensions as irrelevant or unimportant. Great SMEs, however, broaden their vision and hone their skills three-dimensionally.

5

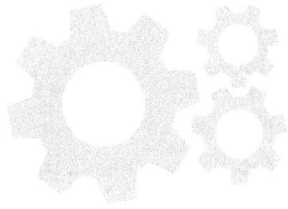

EXPERT PERFORMANCE

According to the academic literature, expert performance occurs when there are "superior reproducible performances on representative tasks within a respective domain."[2] This scholarly definition implies, among other things, that expert performance is measured. In fact, it must be. There could be no "superior reproducible performance" if the performance was not measured in the first place.

Professional athletes, for example, are some of the most measured professionals in the world. They are evaluated every time they compete. Similarly, artists and entertainers are evaluated whenever they stand in front of a microphone. News anchors are evaluated through their broadcasts, and politicians every time they give a speech.

For corporate SMEs, however, the metrics for evaluation are elusive. There are no well-defined playing fields or stages. Measurement of an expert performance might occur at a client meeting or when a supervisor gives a difficult assignment. And few things in life are precisely repeatable. One thing, however, is certain: There will be times when you will be expected to deliver "superior reproducible performance."

When someone is given the title of "subject matter expert," that person is simultaneously challenged to perform in an expert manner and to measure up to a high standard in their field. Singers, baseball players, and other entertainers have a distinct advantage over corporate SMEs in this regard. Entertainers typically know when they are being measured and when they are not. They know when they step onto a stage that they are expected to perform at a high level, but when they are in the practice studio, they know they can relax or at least practice without judgment. Corporate SMEs, on the other hand, frequently do not know when they are being evaluated, or worse, they don't believe they are being evaluated at all.

SMEs can pretend that their performance is not being measured, but it is. It is being measured every time the SME performs. SMEs are best served by identifying the domain of their expertise, understanding the metrics of performance, and then consistently excelling in the representative tasks that define it. This is *expert performance*.

6

DOMAIN OF EXPERTISE

All experts have a domain of competence. Sometimes the domain is well defined and understood, but other times not so much. Professional athletes, for example, have standardized metrics for high performance. For most corporate experts, the situation is different. These experts, such as physicists, psychiatrists, accountants, and engineers, operate in a veritable stew of expectations. It can take years of trial and error for experts in these domains to understand the full scope of their professions. They gradually develop skills and knowledge as needs arise, and they atrophy skills and knowledge that are unneeded.

Corporate division of labor has been the single biggest contributor to the development of expert domains in the past one hundred years. Through division of labor, worker productivity has gone up, repetitive tasks have been streamlined, and low-value tasks have been assigned to lesser-skilled workers. Most expert domains are the byproduct of corporate division of labor.

EXPERT DOMAIN PERSPECTIVES

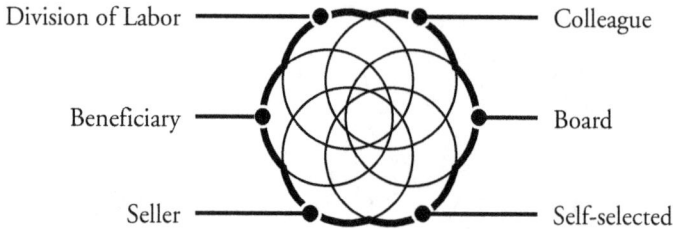

Division of Labor ——————————— Colleague

Beneficiary ——————————— Board

Seller ——————————— Self-selected

Beyond the division of labor, there are other important perspectives that help define each expert domain. Each perspective is worthy of an SME's consideration.

Beneficiary Perspective. Someone should benefit from an expert's actions. A heart attack patient is the beneficiary of a cardiovascular surgeon. A music fan is the beneficiary of an artist. A company is the beneficiary of a tax accountant. All beneficiaries have expectations about the expert's knowledge, skill, and attitude. The beneficiary anticipates that the expert will satisfy a specific set of needs. From the beneficiary's perspective, nothing else matters. Other abilities possessed by the expert are superfluous.

Seller Perspective. Experts, above all others, are uniquely positioned to be masters at selling. Not "selling," as in closing deals, but selling ideas, influencing an audience, or nudging, convincing, and encouraging behavior. Experts are always involved in selling.

Colleague Perspective. Few people will influence an expert more than their colleagues. High-performers should always lift the skills of the people around them. If a corporate SME is surrounded by talented, capable professionals, then the SME will also be a talented and capable professional. It is worth considering what your colleagues expect of you.

Board Perspective. Most expert domains have outside groups that establish standards, develop best practices, and even make laws that govern expert performance. Bar associations govern the actions of lawyers. The American Medical Association defines physicians' specialties. Some boards are formal and powerful. They grant or rescind credentials and may even impose punishment for noncompliance. Other boards are informal and toothless. Regardless, boards can provide SMEs with objective validation and the basis for transferability within their given domains.

Self-Selected Perspective. Finally, all experts have an individual perspective of their own domain. An SME chooses which areas to study and which skills to practice—and determines through deliberate practice how much of the prospective domain will be mastered and how much will not.

All perspectives listed in this chapter contribute to the size and shape of the domain. Great SMEs accept responsibility for excelling in their domain, and this excellence is defined as the union of all contributing factors and perspectives.

7

DIVISION OF LABOR

If companies do not change and improve, they will eventually be replaced. And if experts do not change and improve, they too will eventually be replaced.

As discussed in the previous chapter, one of the most profound ways a company can improve its organizational efficiency is through the division of labor. Division of labor is the assignment of different parts of a process to different people in order to improve overall efficiency. All experts are influenced by, and should consider the implications of, the division of labor on their career and personal performance.

How can your expertise be subdivided, reorganized, redistributed, or outsourced? What are the low-value-added tasks that someone of lesser skill could perform? Tasks that can be done by others should be done by others. Tasks that need to be done by the expert should be done by the expert. Tasks that cannot be done at all should be left in the hands of the experts to figure out. SMEs must always stay ahead of the constantly changing division of labor.

8

DOMAIN TRANSFER

Michael Jordan is one of basketball's all-time greatest players. In 1993, to the surprise of many, he retired from the National Basketball Association (NBA) and attempted to apply his athletic skills to the sport of baseball. Some pundits wondered if Jordan could become as dominant in baseball as he had been in basketball. After he spent one year in baseball's minor leagues, the answer was a clear no. It was evident that Jordan was not going to make the All-Star Team in baseball anytime soon.

In 1995 Jordan returned to the NBA, which was his domain of expertise. In the three years that followed, he led the league in scoring and guided the Chicago Bulls to three consecutive national championships.

Simply stated, expertise is nontransferable. Becoming an expert in one domain does not make a person an expert in another. Rarely can a person rise to the highest ranks of dominance in one field and then quickly replicate that dominance in an entirely different domain. Studies have shown that skill and knowledge in one area seldom qualify a person for excellence in a second domain.[3]

The implications of this may be obvious, but they are worthy of mention. Just because an expert can perform open heart surgery does not mean they can fly an airplane. Just because an expert can configure a web server so that it is impervious to hackers does not mean they can design a microprocessor. And just because an expert can perform brilliantly on the Broadway stage does not mean they are proficient at politics or public policy.

Of course, the opposite is also true. Expertise in one domain does not automatically preclude expertise in another. Given enough time and practice, Michael Jordan may have become a world-class baseball player. We simply do not know. A heart surgeon can learn to fly an airplane and a web security expert can learn to design microprocessors. Expertise in one domain does not mean people should automatically grant you homage in a different domain, but it also doesn't rule out expertise in another. Just because expertise does not automatically transfer doesn't mean that it cannot be replicated.[4]

9

PRACTICE AND PASSION

In 2008 Malcolm Gladwell's book *Outliers* was published by Little, Brown and Company. The book quickly gained notoriety and became a *New York Times* best seller. In the book Gladwell listed many common attributes of highly successful people (the "Outliers," if you will), but the concept that caught the most interest was his "10,000-hour rule." Based on the research of Dr. K. Anders Ericsson, the rule states that top performance in any field requires ten thousand hours of deliberate practice.

Gladwell summarized the rule this way: "Ten thousand hours is the magic number of greatness." The book pointed to the Beatles, Bill Gates, and others as examples of greatness that was achieved when the 10,000-hour rule was satisfied.

In the years that followed the book's publication, many celebrities, athletes, and professionals parroted Gladwell's pithy gem of wisdom. For example, Major League Baseball (MLB) star Alex Rodriguez said, "You first need to acquire your ten thousand hours."[5] Oprah Winfrey chimed in, "I love the theory that there are ten thousand hours behind anybody who ever gets to be successful."[6]

Ericsson, who authored the original research that was the foundation of Gladwell's rule, wrote a thorough response to Gladwell. In Ericsson's book *Peak: Secrets from the New Science of Expertise*, he wrote, "No, the 10,000-hour rule isn't really a rule . . . It is wrong. There is nothing special or magical about 10,000 hours." Ericsson then added, "Gladwell did get one thing right . . .

becoming accomplished in any field in which there is a tremendous amount of effort exerted over many years. It may not require exactly ten thousand hours, but it will take a lot."[7]

Further research confirmed Ericsson's assertion that top performance requires a lot of effort. And the most efficient route is through what Ericsson calls "deliberate practices." (More on that later.) The amount of effort depends on the individual, but there does not appear to be a shortcut. Consider music as an example. Researchers have found that the finest violinists have spent somewhere between 2,894, and 11,926 hours practicing their craft before reaching the top 5 percent. In chess, some people attain grandmaster status in just three thousand hours of practice, while others require twenty-three thousand hours of practice or more.[8]

Regardless of the number of hours invested, greatness requires much more than ordinary persistence, grit, or leaning in. The top experts are obsessed with what they do and how they do it. They don't get tired of practicing, and practicing doesn't make them tired. They persevere, persevere, persevere.

10

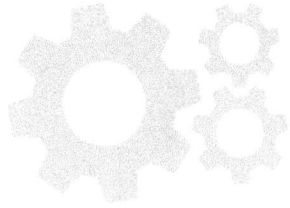

ANECDOTE: PRACTICE AND PASSION

I once knew a physics student who attended a renowned university. The student's father was the dean of the Department of Physics at the same university. At the end of a calculus class, the son visited his father's office in search of assistance. The father patiently explained a complex mathematical concept to his son and asked, "Didn't your professor cover this idea in your class earlier in the semester?"

"Yes, Dad, it was covered."

The father then asked, "And you have not mastered this idea since then?"

"No, Dad, I have not mastered this concept."

The father then approached his son, looked him squarely in the eye, and asked, "When you walk across campus, when you put your head on your pillow at night, when you eat breakfast in the morning, when you don't have anything else to think about, don't you think about calculus?"

The son paused, knowing that his answer would disappoint his physics-loving father. "Umm. No, Dad, I don't," he said.

"Well then, son, you need to find another major. Until you find a subject that captures your curiosity and consumes your interest, you will not master that subject. Now, go discover what you love, and love what you discover."

Eventually, the son received a PhD in Business.

11

RECOGNIZING
AN EXPERT

Experts must give their audience reason to believe they are experts. It seems so obvious that it shouldn't require discussion, but it is too often missed. Every time you interact with an audience, whether an audience of one or an audience of many, that interaction will include an assessment of your expertise. Your audience will be performing a mini-interview, of sorts. And as a result, their faith in you will either grow or diminish. They will either trust your expertise a little more or a little less. Expert interactions rarely end with a neutral assessment.

During those interactions, your audience will be using a simple method to test your expertise. They will be unconsciously asking themselves if the things you espouse as truth reconcile with their opinions: "Given what I know about this subject, can I believe this person?" Their assessment will always start and end from their own point of reference.

It does not matter if your audience has opinions that are right or wrong. They will always assume their starting position is correct. From there, they will attempt to reconcile your words and actions with their own position. If your position does not square with theirs, they will try to reject you rather than rejecting their own preconceived opinion.

Because your audience is always starting and ending the dialogue from their own prejudiced position, you need to quickly position your expertise inside their world. As an expert, your job is to discover where your audience lives mentally and then expand that living space to include the benefits you can provide.

To better understand your audience's perspective, you should speak only after listening to them first. Once you do, you will have greater clarity and fluency in your thoughts and speech, and you will have more power to persuade and convince. When you artfully persuade and convince people about things they did not already know, but which align with their previous knowledge, you will be recognized by them as an expert.

12

CONFIDENCE

Years ago, I met with the chief marketing officer of a publicly traded technology company. I asked him his opinion about SMEs. "You've observed a lot of SMEs in front of clients," I said. "What is it that makes some SMEs great?"

"Confidence!" He answered instantly.

"That's it?" I responded.

"Yep, that's it. Confidence! Hands down! When it comes to client engagement, nothing else comes close."

"You seem rather confident about that," I responded.

"I am!" He then added, "When I meet with clients, I would much rather have a moderately skilled SME with me who brims with confidence than a top-skilled engineer who demonstrates doubt or hesitation. Yep, confidence, hands down."

People trust confidence. They don't trust fear, doubt, weakness, or uncertainty.

Confidence, of course, is belief in yourself. It is the byproduct of knowledge, skill, and most importantly, attitude. People can sense if SMEs believe in themselves. They can feel it. Confidence, or lack thereof, is obvious even before an SME speaks. Confidence is visible in their gait, their posture, their head movement, and their eye contact. Confident people are patient and composed. They are not easily offended or slighted. Great SMEs are confident SMEs.

Yep, confidence, hands down.

13

ANECDOTE: CONFIDENCE

I once attended a meeting with ten highly capable technology professionals. On one side of the table were five representatives from a medium-sized technology vendor. They included an account manager, a sales director, a sales vice president, and two SMEs. On the other side of the table was the chief technology officer (CTO) of a major telecommunications (telco) company and members of his staff.

It was a textbook solution-selling scenario. The vendor sent five of its best and brightest people across the country to woo the telco representatives and convince them to buy the vendor's services. The vendor team was well prepared for their one chance to make a good impression on the telco executives.

At the beginning of the meeting, the account manager tried to give a carefully crafted PowerPoint presentation, but the telco executives would have no part of it. Instead, the CTO began bombarding the vendor's representatives with questions. At first, the questions were high level. They focused on organizational fit and market opportunities. Quickly, however, the focus shifted from high-level strategy to low-level technology. The entire telco team quizzed the vendor team, looking for holes in the solution. Eventually, the sales representatives from the vendor were left out of the conversation. The meeting became a conversation between the telco CTO and the two vendor SMEs. It was a classic high-stakes technology joust.

The SMEs served their company well. They answered questions about architecture, scaling, high availability, integration, intellectual property, code management, and more. The SMEs responded to questions with confidence and candor. They asked for clarifications when the CTO was vague, and they tactfully cleared up misunderstandings. As an observer, I was impressed with the SMEs' performance.

Eventually, the CTO started grilling the SMEs about security. The CTO did not waste time with easy questions he knew the SMEs could answer. He assumed they would take care of the basics. Instead, the CTO jumped right to the newest and most speculative vulnerabilities. He asked something like, "What are you doing to protect against quantum?"

The SMEs could not do anything to protect against quantum vulnerabilities because the entire concept was academic; it was theoretical. The very idea of quantum vulnerability was new and speculative. The CTO knew this vendor could not solve for quantum, and the CTO also knew that there were no legitimate security threats from quantum computing. But what the CTO did not know, and what he was seeking to learn, was the erudition of the SMEs. Were they informed about the current scholarship within their industry? Could he trust the SMEs to stay ahead of the industry trends? If quantum or other vulnerabilities should arise, would they be prepared?

When the CTO asked the question, I watched as both SMEs subtly but discernably dropped their heads. They did not have an answer for the CTO's question, and they knew it. With a primal instinct, they lowered their heads in submission to the dominant CTO who asked the question. They stammered for a moment, talked briefly about internal security policies, and quickly transitioned to another subject. There was almost an audible "gotcha" in the room. The meeting ended and the vendor did not secure the business of the telecommunications company, primarily because of that moment when the SMEs showed a lack of confidence.

Great SMEs don't drop their head. They keep eye contact, even when it's hard to do. They keep their head up and answer questions with confidence. If they must say, "I don't know," then they do it with their chin up and their shoulders back. Remember, great SMEs are confident, and confidence is never conveyed while staring at the floor.

14

MORE ABOUT CONFIDENCE

William Osler, a cofounder of Johns Hopkins Hospital, once opined that, "Medicine is a science of uncertainty and an art of probability."[9] Medical doctors, like other experts, will experience periods of hesitation and doubt. They know their efforts will not always produce a positive outcome. Yet, despite the risks and uncertainties of their craft, they know that sick patients need confident physicians.

Patients who have faith in their doctors are more likely to listen to them and abide by their council. Patients who do not trust their doctors, on the other hand, are less likely to take prescribed medications or follow advice about behavioral changes. This is a big problem in medicine—studies show that especially with long-term treatments, patients comply with medical directions less than 50 percent of the time.[10]

Medical treatment adherence is a multifaceted problem, with patient confidence being just one important factor.[11] Patients need to have confidence in their physicians, yet many doctors project uncertainty, which sabotages the confidence that their patients need. Without even thinking about it, doctors might use phrases like, "my guess is," "I'm not sure," "let's see what happens," or "I haven't seen that before." Doctors and all other experts should project confidence and certainty, rather than hesitation or doubt.

I am occasionally told that statements of uncertainty from doctors are simple honesty, and that honesty is far better than false confidence. This may be true, and it goes without saying that all experts should be honest and forthcoming. But it is possible to be honest and confident at the same time. Yet, many experts place too much emphasis on uncertainty and risk.

Medical literature shows that doctors often underestimate the damage they inflict on their patients by making doubtful or uncertain statements.[12] It is no more honest for an expert to scare a patient about an obscure risk than it is to ignore the risk altogether. The role of the expert is to understand all aspects of a preferred treatment and then propose that treatment with confidence and conviction.[13]

15

CURSE OF KNOWLEDGE

I always hated the game charades as a boy. For those who are unfamiliar with charades, it is when one person tries to help their teammates guess a short phrase using only pantomime. From my very first experience with the game, I thought it was a ridiculous exercise. If you know the title of a book or a song, then just say it. Why intentionally complicate communications with artificial constraints? Furthermore, I realized that the hearing impaired already had sign language that solves for nonverbal communication. To the hearing impaired, charades must seem completely ridiculous. I could not share in the fun that other people experienced because I found the game irrational.

Years later, I discovered that expertise brings with it a permanent form of charades. You know something that other people do not know, and they do not share a vocabulary with you, which is an obstacle to communication. Knowledge is a curse in charades. What is clear and obvious to you is neither clear nor obvious to your audience, and you both lack the communication tools necessary to bridge the knowledge divide.

The curse of knowledge is one of the biggest challenges for SMEs. They often assume that other people understand them, follow their reasoning, and will arrive at the same logical conclusions as them. This mental bias of assumptions influences the way experts communicate. When you know something, it can be difficult to pretend you don't, and it can be difficult to remember what it was like before you knew it. Once they master a subject, experts quickly forget the struggles they experienced gaining the knowledge. Researchers have known for decades that knowledge can create communication problems.[14] In his book *The Sense of Style*, Steven Pinker indicates that "the main cause of incomprehensible prose is the difficulty of imagining what it's like for someone else not to know something that you know."[15]

There are, of course, many things you as an SME can do to remedy the curse of knowledge. First, you must recognize it exists. If you do not realize that people cannot understand you, then you won't be able to help them. People do not want to appear stupid or uninformed, so they often disguise their confusion and pretend to understand. You should avoid complicated phraseology, jargon, and acronyms (more on that later). Don't assume that everyone knows what your words mean. Even adding a few words to an explanation can be enormously helpful.

Recognizing that your abstractions are not their abstractions is also important. Your audience has not studied your subject for years or decades the way you have. Consequently, they do not put things in the same buckets or sort things in the same order. As an expert, you should take nothing for granted. Speak to the least informed person in the room and use plain language. Don't assume they understand you even when they say they do.

Don't get frustrated with the game of charades. It can be painful when things go wrong, but you don't have a better choice. You can either bridge the communication divide that accompanies knowledge, or you can speak over the heads of your audience and minimize your effectiveness.

16

ANECDOTE: CURSE OF KNOWLEDGE

Several years ago, my son and I planned to watch a basketball game on television. The Boston Celtics were playing the Miami Heat in Game 4 of the NBA Eastern Conference Finals. To my son's disappointment, he had a school obligation that conflicted with the game. No problem, we thought, we'll just DVR the game and watch it when we get home. To maintain suspense, my son and I both turned off our smartphones to avoid any media alerts. My wife stayed home for the evening and watched the Celtics win in overtime.

When we arrived home, my wife innocently said to us, "You guys are going to enjoy the game!"

"Mom!?!" My son reacted with disappointment, "You just wrecked it!"

Attempting to backtrack, she responded, "I didn't say the Celtics won, I just said you will enjoy it."

"Well then, obviously they won," my son responded. "I'm not going to enjoy it if the Celtics lost! You completely wrecked it!" He was incensed and stomped out of the room, then went to bed in a huff without watching one minute of the recorded game.

The experience was a reminder to me that things can change the instant you learn something new, even if what you learn is a trivial detail. As my son's reaction attests, it's impossible to watch a basketball game with the same anticipation if the outcome is known. Similarly, it's difficult to watch a movie with the same interest and curiosity if a friend or critic has spoiled the plot. When we learn something, our emotions change, our expectations change, and our perceptions change. And once we learn something, we can't unlearn it. We might eventually forget it, but we can't go back in time and accurately see things with the same eye or hear things with the same ear that we once did. Everything changes permanently with knowledge.

This concept is particularly important for SMEs because they know things other people do not know, and they cannot put themselves into a state of not knowing. The gap of knowledge between the expert and the layperson is often a source of tremendous frustration and distrust. It is incumbent on the SME to empathize with people. SMEs must deliberately try to put themselves in their audiences' shoes and remember the difficulty they had learning their domain for the first time.

CHALLENGES

17

TIMES ARE CHANGING

Being a subject matter expert today is more difficult than it was ten years ago and far more difficult than twenty years ago. In just a few decades, less time than it takes to navigate a full career, the entire concept of expertise has shifted. We have gone from viewing experts as talented and sought-after sources of power and influence to viewing them as either arrogant or irrelevant.

During the 2016 presidential campaign, Donald Trump summarized the mood of many when he said, "You know, I've always wanted to say this—I've never said this before . . . The experts are terrible."[16] He was not alone in his criticism. In 2017 Dr. Tom Nichols of the US Naval War College (and no fan of Donald Trump, by the way) wrote an entire book about the plight of expertise. In it, Nichols said, "I fear we are witnessing the death of the ideal of expertise itself."[17] Two years later, *Washington Monthly* magazine enumerated an intentional and systematic purge of experts from the federal government.[18]

While I do not share former President Trump's view nor Tom Nichols' pessimism, I agree with a growing sentiment that SMEs are underappreciated and, more important, depreciating in value. Being an SME is hard and getting harder.

Many forces are at work against SMEs, and they are multiplying steadily. Each factor individually can be addressed and overcome, but their combined influence is material and growing. They combine to buffet the SME at every turn. In this section we will outline several of the challenges facing SMEs. A few years from now the list will undoubtedly be different and longer. Let's start with the biggies.

18

TECHNOLOGY

Computers are encroaching on human experts in every subject and discipline, and they will continue to do so at an accelerating pace. As computer proficiency increases, trust in human expertise diminishes. Google has been the default knowledge authority for decades. This alone has reduced the dependency on experts. Every time someone says, "Google it," they are saying that technology is a more reliable source of information on that subject at that moment than any available person.

Technology has many distinct advantages over human experts. For example, people get tired and go to sleep, but technology is always alert, always on, and always available. People can be in only one place at one time, but technology is omnipresent. People can do only one thing at a time and serve only one audience at a time, but technology scales infinitely. People make mistakes and are inconsistent, but technology gets the same answer every time. People forget, but technology remembers. People are cruel, but technology is impartial. People die, but technology is immortal.

19

SHELF LIFE

When food stays on the shelf past its expiration date, it is considered unsalable and unfit for consumption. The same is true for expertise and expert performance; these always have an expiration date.

Food producers have known for centuries that four factors determine how long perishable products will retain their freshness: 1) the formulation of the food, 2) the processes used in production, 3) the packaging, and 4) the storage conditions. These four things define the expiration. Any change or variability in these factors will impact shelf life.

Expertise and expert performance can be seen through a similar lens: 1) They have a formulation and means of production; 2) They are packaged and stored; 3) Consequently, they have a shelf life; and 4) They do not last forever. They are only good for so long.

All four of these factors are being buffeted. The formulation of expertise is changing. What constituted expertise a few years ago does not necessarily constitute expertise today. The path and means of production are changing. Does an SME need a bachelor's degree or even a PhD—or maybe no degree at all? The packaging of an SME is changing. What does an expert look like, sound like, or act like? And, of course, the means of storing expertise is changing dramatically as well. Must expertise be captured in a blog or a YouTube video? And if it is, when does it expire?

Food producers have made tremendous strides in extending the shelf life of our perishable foods. They have tweaked and adjusted all four key factors that determine it. SMEs, on the other hand, are becoming increasingly perishable. The raw ingredients and means of production of expertise are plentiful. The packaging is endless and the storage infinite.

Rarely do SMEs consider their own shelf life, but one thing is certain: Whatever an SME's shelf life was a decade ago, or even a year ago, it has changed since then. What to do? You can expand your shelf life with better formulation, more effective production, compelling packaging, and improved storage.

20

CONTENT VOLUME

The amount of data produced in the world is staggering. We perform billions of searches per day. We watch billions of videos. We upload billions of images and posts. We receive billions of spam emails. We send billions of text messages. We swipe, like, and tweet constantly. We can say almost anything and have it shared globally, instantly. And all these things are becoming easier and easier to perform by more and more connected people. The sheer volume of available information is mind-blowing.

In contrast, the work of an SME is not getting easier, at least not at the same pace. Uncovering new truths remains a laborious task. Ask anyone who creates peer-reviewed scientific papers for serious journals and they will tell you that publishing a paper with new information is hard work. It is tedious and time-consuming, and yet it rarely gets much attention.

Consequently, the sheer disproportionality of fluff to facts and subjectivity to objectivity is lopsided and trending further and further toward the unproductive, insignificant, and pointless. The sheer volume of meaningless content consumes more and more of our days, leaving little time for the SME to make a point or convince a doubter. The volume of content is trending against the SME and that trend grows larger and larger every day.

21

MEMORY OUTSOURCING

For much of humankind's evolutionary history, we could only store memories in our own minds. Eventually, we developed written language that allowed us to record a few important events for future generations.

Nearly five thousand years passed after written language was developed before the Gutenberg press was invented. The printing press enabled memory outsourcing on an industrial scale. Between the fifteenth and eighteenth centuries, the number of books produced in Europe grew from a few million volumes to nearly one billion copies.[19]

Fast forward a few centuries, and we now live in a time when the internet and mobile technologies have dramatically accelerated memory outsourcing. Every word and image, every event, and every conversation can now be recorded forever. What is said to one person in an isolated hut on one side of the world can be retrieved instantaneously on the other side of the globe. These advancements in memory outsourcing have brought many benefits to the human family, but they have also brought grievous liabilities. Minor indiscretions or lapses in judgment now live forever. A private conversation can be stored and broadcast endlessly. Confidential and personal information is stolen routinely.

Researchers have long known that expertise is, among other things, the byproduct of enhanced memory and efficient memory management. The more memories you have in a domain, the more of an expert you can become. And the more effectively you manage your memory with cognitive skills, the more your memories enhance your performance. Of course, the opposite is also true: without memory, there is no expertise or expert performance. Memories make or break experts.

The free distribution of memory is one of the largest challenges for SMEs in all domains. Today, unlike at any other time, memory and its management are being outsourced and distributed. Memories that once signified an expert's knowledge and performance are now being uploaded and distributed to every interested person on the planet. The result is the commoditization of expertise and the rapid entry of competitors.

SMEs now more than ever must use technology to enhance and upload their memories. They must remain aware of the memories of others, and they must continue to develop memories that differentiate themselves from others.

Memory outsourcing cannot be slowed. It will expand and accelerate. Today's SMEs must seek out the memories of others, contribute to the memories of their domains, and leverage every available resource for managing memories. They also need to access memories more quickly and accurately than at any other time. The time may be coming when experts are not distinguished by the memories they store in their own minds. Instead, they will be known for their ability to manage the memories of themselves and others.

22

POST-TRUTH ERA

Truth is the only meaningful foundation upon which people can make informed and rational decisions. Therefore, truth is the SME's currency. The more truth an SME possesses, the more influence they can exert and the longer lasting their influence and appeal.

Truth, it turns out, is stubborn and stable. It is blind, fearless, and timeless. Truth does not care about feelings or opinions. It does not bend to political power, societal norms, cultural preferences, or social whims. Truth just is.

Without truth an SME has nothing of lasting value. Without truth they have only theatrical performance or a cardboard façade. Truth is the SME's primary source of lasting power, authority, weight, and control. Yet, despite the universal influence of truth and the dogged persistence of it, truth is now losing popularity. It is falling out of fashion. It is no longer cool. Truth is old school.

The 2016 Oxford Dictionaries word of the year was *post-truth*. Many argue that we now live in a post-truth era: a time when objective facts are less influential in shaping opinion and public policy than appeals to emotion and personal belief. The appeal of emotion over fact is hardly new. Marketing professionals have known for a very long time that emotions sell products much more quickly than facts. But in our ultraconnected world, more and more messages want to be heard. The way these messages become heard is through heightened emotion. Emotion is pushing truth further and further aside.

This trend away from truth and toward the outrageous and extreme is having an impact on SMEs. They no longer have the luxury of depending on truth alone. The truths that might have won an argument in yesteryear may no longer be enough to win the argument today. Of course, truth still matters—it always will—but SMEs now need more than just truth to maintain relevance.

In a post-truth era, SMEs need charisma and presence to maximize their impact. Of course, they still need the skills that other people do not have, but they also need the professional appeal that other people admire. The best experts can wrap truth in an attractive package, top it off with a bow, and deliver it in digestible portions.

We may live in a post-truth era, but truth still matters.

23

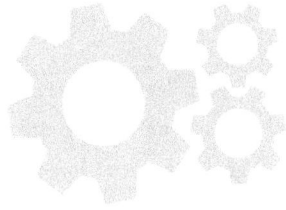

FACTS ARE AGGRESSIVE

F acts are the indispensable tools of SMEs. They are always consistent with objective reality, and they can be proven through evidence. They are foundational and the basis of logical inference. They do not bend for the rich or the powerful. They are rarely delicate. They can be painful and difficult, heavy and hard. Facts are often uncomfortable to speak and distressing to hear.

Experience has taught me that some SMEs depend solely on the power of facts to exercise their influence. They swing facts like clubs, wear facts like armor, and crown their heads with fact-fashioned headgear. These SMEs are injurious, impervious, and intimidating, all at the same time. They attempt to crush falsehoods and dismantle flimsy philosophies. They find great joy in the facts that support them and care little for the wreckage that those facts can leave in their wake. They subscribe to the philosophy of author and philosopher Ayn Rand, who said, "If the truth shall kill them, let them die."[20]

In vivid contrast to the fact-clinching SME, we have a large and growing public awash in post-truth thinking. These days our culture cares more for feelings than facts. We protect the hypersensitive as if they were oppressed, and we cocoon the delicate feelings of the offended. If language offends then it must be rejected. If a fact causes discomfort, then a safe space must be provided. We emphasize manufactured outrage and make celebrities of victims, both real and imagined.

Facts still rule the day, as they always will, but the days are over when simple facts alone will win the debate, much less calm a troubled heart or silence a frightened crowd. It is increasingly likely that winning a debate will be considered hostile and mean-spirited. Of course, experts must embrace facts no matter how difficult, no matter how painful. To act otherwise would be ruinous to their recommendations, their knowledge, and their skills. But facts can be painful and aggressive. In a post-truth era, an SME is expected to walk the tightrope between truth and sensitivity, facts and feelings.

24

MOUNT STUPID IS EASILY CLIMBED

It is a truth of human nature that as soon as most people obtain a little knowledge on a subject, they immediately assume they are wise and begin to wield their knowledge presumptuously. People with a little knowledge often become proud, arrogant, and condescending. They place themselves on par with or even above the truly informed, gifted, and expert. As William Shakespeare once wrote, "The fool doth think he is wise, but the wise man knows himself to be a fool."[21]

This phenomenon of illusory superiority is called "Mount Stupid." It would be nice if the smug folks who scale Mount Stupid discovered that there is far more to be learned than what a ten-minute internet search can possibly reveal. With luck, the cocky pretenders would eventually be humbled, rethink their preconceptions, and place themselves among the novices and beginners where they rightfully belong. But, alas, this type of luck is not to be. No matter where we are on the path to expertise, we almost always judge ourselves to be more qualified, skilled, and informed than we actually are.

The problem we now face, unlike just a few years ago, is that the path up Mount Stupid is well marked and easily traveled. There was a time when gaining cursory knowledge of a subject required the seekers to peruse a book at the local library or to telephone a well-informed friend. It now takes just a few seconds to obtain the knowledge that used to require days or weeks. As a result, superficial knowledge is now accessible to everyone everywhere all the time, which means that more people occupy Mount Stupid than at any other time in human history.

Because Mount Stupid is so easily accessible, SMEs no longer interact with people who are innocently uninformed. Instead, they interface with people who are often arrogantly superficial. The only thing harder for an SME than interacting with an audience that has no knowledge about their subject is interacting with an audience that knows just a little bit about their subject. Welcome to the observation deck facing Mount Stupid.

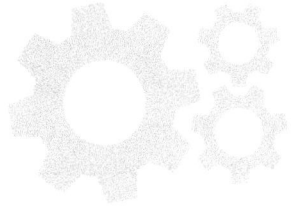

25

MEMBERSHIP

Americans are taught that independence from Great Britain came at the end of the eighteenth century, as a result of the colonial revolt against the British Empire. The rebellion was motivated by martial law, trade restrictions, taxation, unfair representation, and more. The Boston Tea Party was in 1773, the Declaration of Independence was signed in 1776, and the Constitution was signed in 1787. It was a busy period for the fledgling United States.

One thing we don't often find in history books is that the American Revolution was, in small part, also a revolt against institutional expertise. The pre-revolution experts had power and influence. The colonials resented the elitist guilds and the monopolistic controls they exerted. After the revolution, most laws requiring professional certification in the United States were systematically eliminated. For example, between the 1840s and the 1890s, there was no requirement for certification to practice medicine or law in the United States.[22]

In the twentieth century, professional certifications returned, and licenses were required once again to practice these and many other professions. Doctors, dentists, lawyers, financial advisors, and electricians now must get certified and be members of a sanctioned association. This protects the public from malpractice. It ensures a verified level of proficiency and establishes a baseline for legal accountability.

Being certified in a field is also a social signal. It is a message to others that you are important. In many domains, membership in an elite group bestows legitimacy. For example, if you are a Nobel Prize recipient, you are a member of an exclusive group. Membership in that group bestows, or at least testifies, to your expertise. The same can be said for anyone who receives an Oscar nomination or who plays basketball in the NBA.

While membership often signifies endorsement, it may also bestow trust. If you are a certified public accountant, for example, you are frequently assumed to be trustworthy and knowledgeable. There are, of course, violators of this trust, but the American Institute of CPAs works diligently to maintain the CPA brand, and because of its vigilance, CPAs reap benefits, financially and otherwise.

Great SMEs become members of the right groups, societies, and associations. Even in professions where the value of such membership is ambiguous, they find and influence the associations that govern their field.

Most people believe that trade associations maintain standards, and those standards are used to define who is considered an expert. But great SMEs know it works the other way around. They define the standards, which are in turn used to define and measure their discipline. An SME can either act or be acted upon. Great SMEs act.

It is unlikely that we will ever return to the 1840s when membership in a professional organization did not matter. To the contrary, most professions will see an increasing emphasis on membership and certification. It is in an SME's best interest to become a member and set the standards for themself and others.

26

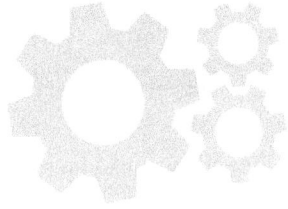

NEW JOURNALISM

Once upon a time, journalists were the ultimate authorities. They selected the stories, they conducted the research, they wrote the articles, they held the microphones, they pointed the cameras, and they controlled the papers and the broadcast towers. Journalists shaped, or at least influenced, public opinion and narrative. Today, however, the traditional journalist is disappearing. Now anyone can be a contributing writer, commentator, or pundit. Anyone can espouse their opinion. Anyone can be an expert or pretend to be one.

We now live in a twenty-four-hour news cycle when content cannot be created too quickly and news outlets race to be first with a story. There is so much information of all types that we gravitate toward the familiar and the reassuring. We don't read to be taught anymore; we now read to be validated. The most popular sources of news are now marinated with entertainment and drama to increase appeal. Yet, trust in media is at an all-time low. Cries of "fake news" abound.

It would be convenient if SMEs could ignore the shifting sands of journalism and dismiss the trend as irrelevant. But SMEs are experiencing many of same challenges that reporters are facing, with the only difference being that the challenges are less obvious for SMEs.

Trends in technology, consumer preferences, and popular behavior influence SMEs and journalists alike. From an SME's perspective, the journalist is simply the canary in the coal mine. If the air is polluted for the journalist, then the air is also polluted for the SME. If someone is critical or distrusting of journalism, then they are probably critical or distrusting of SMEs as well. If consumers don't have patience for long-winded articles, then they probably don't have patience for long-winded explanations from SMEs either.

Today's SMEs need to take a page from journalism. Modern consumers of information don't want data served dry, cold, and brittle. They don't want to wait two minutes for something that can be served in one. They don't want to smell condescension in the air or be told that their opinions don't matter. They want to be informed and entertained, educated and inspired. They want what they want, and they are only interested in what you have if it helps them get what they want.

So, learn to give people what they want, at least a little bit. Give them enthusiasm. If SMEs can't be passionate about their field of excellence, then who can? Give people some excitement. If an SME can't show interest and enthusiasm about a subject, then who will? Give people a reason to believe and show them a reason to care.

27

PEOPLE DON'T KNOW THEY'RE WRONG

To be wrong is to believe that something is true when it is actually false, or conversely, to believe something is false when it is actually true. In my experience with SMEs for the past two decades, this is how most of them think about truth and falsity. It is binary. You are right or you are wrong. Truth is empirical and verifiable. Falsity should be avoided because it is at odds with reality.

This factual approach is of course simplistic. A complete definition of the word *wrong* must also include moral and preferential dimensions. From a factual perspective, it may be wrong to think the world is flat. From a moral perspective, it may be wrong to lie or to rob a bank. And from a preferential perspective, it may be wrong to eat apple pie without vanilla ice cream or to indent paragraphs with spaces rather than tabs. All these things are wrong. (At least they are in my judgment.) But some things are more wrong than others.

For some strange reason, which researchers have never quite determined, humans have a difficult time recognizing their own errors.[23] As children, we were told we were wrong frequently. We were corrected by parents, siblings, teachers, coaches, and friends. Over time the frequency of our errors diminished while the seriousness of our errors increased. As adults and professionals, we are still wrong about many things, but fewer people are willing to point it out to us.

In an odd way, most people believe they are omniscient. They go through their days believing they are making the right decisions, spending their time on the right things, interacting with the right people, and obtaining the best possible outcomes. We rarely look back on our days and see the things we did wrong.

No one likes to be wrong. Being wrong can be painful, embarrassing, frightening, confusing, and costly. Learning you were wrong is rarely enjoyable. We now live in a time when many people are sensitive about being told they are wrong; they think it is synonymous with being called stupid. Dealing with wrongness is more precarious now than ever before.

An SME must discover and work through the implications of being wrong. If something seems to be wrong, then the SME should start with themself. Are you, the SME, wrong? If so, own it, correct it, communicate it, and move on. If not, then assume the person who is wrong does not know that they are wrong. Rarely do people recognize their own error. Help them discover deficiencies and improvements. Don't pass judgment, factually, morally, or preferentially. Don't tell people they are wrong, but instead gracefully and tactfully show them where progress is possible.

Sometimes the truth is painful, and SMEs need to be willing to expose painful things, but most of the time they can correct with a tone of empathy, encouragement, patience, and love. Being wrong is hard, so don't make it harder. Lighten the load and share the burden of being wrong.

28

EXPERTS ARE FREQUENTLY WRONG

When an SME is wrong, trust dissolves and dissension follows, not just for the expert in question, but for all experts who come after. So, don't be wrong. Don't go out on limbs. Don't pontificate on subjects you haven't adequately studied. It can be tempting to expound when asked, but don't do it if there's a chance you'll be mistaken.[24]

Of course, not being wrong is not the same as always being right. Experts don't have to be right in every instance. It would be impossible for experts to be correct in every detail and in every instance. We all make mistakes, but in my observation, experts can avoid being wrong a lot more than they do.

The two easiest ways to avoid being wrong are to exercise caution when making declarative statements and to add the appropriate qualifiers when you do speak. What assumptions are you making that give you confidence in your declarative statements? How likely are those assumptions to be true? Unless you know something to be true, don't declare that it is. And when you do declare something to be true, put it in its appropriate box and add the appropriate caution and exceptions.

SOCIAL POWER IS SHIFTING

Technology is enabling a global shift in social power. Decades ago, the typical teenager could be a consumer of entertainment and pop culture, but had zero influence. Now, through a YouTube channel or a SoundCloud account, a teen can create, share, and promote content instantly. Any individual teen can be heard by millions of people, at any time, in any corner of the globe. We have transitioned from a time when the masses were passive recipients of ideas to a time when they are the creators and promoters of their own ideas. Furthermore, teens and others have discovered that their ideas are often as good or better than the ideas promoted by traditional media companies.

In a similar fashion, ride-sharing services like Uber and Lyft have shifted power away from transportation institutions and into the hands of individual vehicle owners. Airbnb has shifted power away from hospitality institutions and into the hands of property owners. Amazon has harnessed consumer spending, enabled individuals to have online storefronts, and decimated the shopping mall. Bloggers have killed the newspapers. Open-source software has placed unprecedented power in the hands of individual software developers. Self-publishing is encroaching on traditional printing processes. And now peer-to-peer financing is chipping away at the oldest of the power institutions, the bank.

Subject matter experts are also subject to shifts in power, for better or worse. In one sense an expert is a cog in the institutional wheel, where power is diminishing. The corporate SME is now just one voice in a sea of diverse sentiments, and in many industries, these experts are automatically doubted, questioned, or rejected. Increasingly, expertise is met with opposition and, at times, hostility. Twenty years ago, being called an expert was a compliment. Now, not as much. The word *expert* is often used sarcastically, or worse, with skepticism. As the corporation goes, so goes the corporate SME.

But SMEs can advance their perspectives in the same fashion as others these days. The tools afforded the teenagers are the same ones available to the SMEs. This does not mean that SMEs should publish songs about their craft on Spotify (please don't), but it does mean that they can become outspoken and independent advocates for their causes. Experts needn't sit back and watch as the power shifts from old centralized institutions to the new decentralized masses. They can and should be leading contributors to the conversation wherever that conversation occurs. Just because power is shifting doesn't mean it must depart from the experts. Great SMEs retain and strengthen their influence in spite of the technology changes that challenge them.[25]

30

NO MORE LOCAL ADVANTAGE

For centuries, expertise was a local endeavor. Experts did not need to be the best in the world, because they did not compete beyond the confines of their narrow markets. An individual did not have to be the absolute best if no one better could be found. But the advent of global transportation and instant communication has caused disruption in the market for experts.[26]

When global competition first appeared, it came in the form of massive factories and cheap labor. Now, competition is reaching every facet of individual performance. Every expert in the world can be known by a global audience.

The customers of expertise no longer look for help within their shire or hamlet as they once did. They can find global experts with no more effort than typing in a search engine. There are no stringent barriers to entry, no lasting import or export constraints, and few enforceable intellectual property protections. The truth is, all experts now compete globally, and all are vulnerable to challenges from every corner of the globe. The days of the local advantage are gone forever.

31

EXPERTS ARE FREQUENTLY IGNORED

Once achieved, expert status is both sweet and sour. It is exhilarating and disappointing simultaneously. At first, a subject matter expert is thrilled when they are sought out for advice or assistance, but soon all experts realize that their recommendations are more likely to be ignored than followed and their achievements are more likely to be passed over than celebrated. An SME is one voice in a sea of opinions and one actor on a massive and crowded stage. People will question an expert's motives, ridicule their credentials, dismiss their advice, or scoff at their accomplishments.

When an expert says something the audience does not like, they will reject that expert and their message, and quickly seek another "expert" who will say or do what they want. David Ben-Gurion was the first prime minister of Israel. He is credited as saying, "If an expert says it can't be done, get another expert."[27] And get another expert they will. This is exactly the sentiment held by many people in many industries: If one expert will not do or say as I wish, there is almost certainly another expert who will.

With the proliferation of skilled people and communications technology, there is almost a guarantee that experts will be ignored. With more and more information comes less and less attention. Experts today are more likely to be ignored than ever before.

32

FAKERS ABOUND

Faking something doesn't make it so.

It is not clear exactly when the phrase "fake it 'til you make it" was introduced into the American lexicon, but it is now a cliché. This pithy statement captures much of what ails many subject matter experts today.

In the 1920s a psychologist named Alfred Adler developed a therapeutic technique he called "acting as if." The concept has now been used for nearly a hundred years by mental health professionals to help patients practice alternatives to dysfunctional behavior. Typically, people can control their actions more easily than they can control their feelings, therefore Adler recommended performing actions as if the feelings had already occurred. He argued that if you act before you feel inclined to do so, the desired feelings will often follow. For example, instead of waiting until you feel happy before you smile, Adler posited that if you smile first, you will begin to feel happy. And, instead of waiting for your confidence to build before you engage with people socially, if you engage socially, then your confidence will build. Adler could be the father of "fake it 'til you make it," even though he did not coin the phrase.

Unfortunately, the application of "fake it 'til you make it" has now gone far beyond the original intent of helping to correct dysfunctional behavior. There is no sin in self-talk or other forms of self-improvement, but faking is now encouraged to the point of blatant dishonesty. Faking is even embraced as justification for deceit or fraud. It is one thing to fake that you are happy when you are not, or to fake that you are socially confident when you are not, but faking competence and expertise is an entirely different thing. Faking that you are an engineer or a physician or a police officer does not make it so.

We now live in a time when people are openly encouraged to act as if they are someone they are not. People have learned that pretending to be an expert can be highly advantageous. Unfortunately, acting like an expert is rarely exposed or prosecuted. This is a shame, because as we discussed previously, gaining expertise is a laborious and tedious process. It requires thousands of hours of dedicated effort, which the faker circumvents.

Faking has always been appealing to many. The difference now is that the benefits can be high and the penalties low. People are encouraged to perpetuate a fraud. They have learned that they are more likely to obtain what they want if they talk long enough, loud enough, or with enough conviction. Faking something doesn't make it so, but it is certainly helping people to get what they want.

33

THIN SLICING

How much time do you need to spend with a person before you're able to make an accurate judgment of their character? How quickly can you decide if the person is an expert? It turns out you don't need much time at all. In many instances, our first impressions are more than enough.

In 1993 researchers videotaped several college instructors while they were teaching. Then they extracted sections of the instructors' presentations—segments of two, five, and, ten seconds long—which they called thin slices. The researchers showed the segments to strangers and asked them to rate each teacher's effectiveness. They compared the strangers' assessments with the traditional teacher assessments given by students at the end of a semester of instruction. Remarkably, the strangers' appraisals of the instructors after just a few seconds of silent video were highly correlated with student assessments after months of interaction.[28]

"Thin slicing," as the phenomenon was dubbed, refers to our ability to view narrow slivers or samples of situations without losing meaning. Thin slicing has been validated and revalidated many times across many disciplines. It applies to job interviews, dating, sales, doctor/patient relations, and more.[29] Out of necessity, people are slicing subject matter experts more and more thinly and passing judgment more and more quickly. As an SME, you are being thinly sliced.

BECOMING AN EXPERT

34

WHY DO IT?

With rare exceptions, becoming an expert in any field takes years of study, practice, and commitment. There is almost never an easy path. Some disciplines take longer than others to master, but the path is neither quick nor simple. The route may seem easy at first, but eventually the slope goes steeply uphill and the lighting becomes dim. And, to be sure, the route is flanked by skeptics. The naysayers can be found at every turn. They mock from every high hill. The process of gaining expertise is so painful, in fact, that many of the most capable people are filtered out because they lack the means or the dedication required. When people mock or point fingers, it is tempting to let go of the goal, wander off the path, and settle for mediocrity.

So why do it? Why commit thousands of hours and endless energy to developing an expertise that might never be fully utilized or appreciated? Why become truly expert at anything? Maybe good enough is good enough.

Some people pursue an expertise as a hobby, some as an obsession, and some as an opportunity. Many people do it because experts earn more money than non-experts, while some use expertise as a path to power, influence, or control. Still others simply crave attention, notoriety, or fame. Some experts go so far as to identify their pursuit as the very purpose of their existence. To them, being an expert is more than the thing they were meant to do; it is the thing that defines who they are.

Whatever inspires you as an expert, be it wealth, fame, power, or something else, those motives will eventually reveal themselves to the people around you. Try as you might, you cannot permanently hide your true motives from the people you influence.

At the end of the day, what really matters is that experts have a greater capacity to serve. Experts can help people in ways that others cannot. Experts can lift, fix, solve, build, and unify where others fail. Becoming an expert is a truly noble pursuit because experts can serve people in ways that they cannot serve themselves. The best experts, the truly inspiring ones, are those who strive first to lift others, even before they lift themselves.

Your influence as an expert will flourish when you know deep down in your gut the true reason for your pursuit. If your expertise is all about your power, your influence, or your control, then your accomplishments will benefit only you. But if your highest priority is to lift and help others, then your accomplishments will be multiplied and accentuated.

Our world is filled with pain, doubt, loneliness, and heartache. Many things need to be changed and improved, and many people need assistance. However, the world is rarely changed by the ordinary, the good enough, or the commonplace. No, changing the world requires experts—people with tremendous capacity, tenacity, strength, and courage. Experts can make a profound difference in the world.

Becoming an expert is one of the most noble of human pursuits. The path is hard, and because it is hard, it brings discipline to action, clarity to thought, and fulfillment to interests. Being an expert can and should be a lifelong pursuit, but it should be done for the right reasons: for the purpose of lifting, helping, and encouraging others. In short, to be a valued expert—a truly great influence in the world—is to be a servant who is motivated by love.

35

DREYFUS AND DREYFUS

In 1980 Stuart and Hubert Dreyfus, researchers from the University of California, Berkeley, published an eighteen-page report for the United States Air Force Office of Scientific Research. In the report the Dreyfus brothers proposed a model for expert development and performance, including stages for skill acquisition and an observation model for said development. They also pointed out the similarities between developing expert performance in chess, learning a foreign language, and flying an aircraft.

In the decades since its publication, the Dreyfus and Dreyfus model has been expanded and revised and received both praise and criticism. The model is not perfect, but it introduces concepts that all experts should consider.

The Dreyfus and Dreyfus model postulates that becoming an expert is more than just gaining knowledge or learning a skill. The model states that there are five fundamental characteristics of expertise and expert performance common to all disciplines and industries. According to the Dreyfus brothers, experts show how they are exceptional in five separate measurable ways:

- Experts are masters of knowledge.

- Experts deliver a consistently high standard of work.

- Experts can work autonomously.

- Experts understand and manage complexity.

- Experts see the overall context.

In the following chapters, we'll discuss each of these traits and outline why each is important.

36

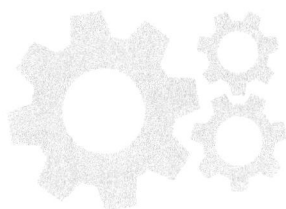

MASTER OF KNOWLEDGE

*"The one thing that I know is
that I know nothing."*

—Socrates

The first true mark of an expert is knowledge. For many people, pursuing expert knowledge is paramount. Expertise, for them, is all about the facts. They focus on verifiable truth, proof, and method, and concentrate on the hypothesis, the observation, and the validation. They believe that wrong ideas will eventually fail, but right ideas will stand forever.

To the knowledge expert, feelings do not matter and opinions are mostly irrelevant. What matters to them is the discovery of things as they really are, and of things as they really will be. To the knowledge expert, power comes from the mastery of details, the accumulation of progressing thoughts, and the layers of proof upon proof.

Paradoxically, the accumulation of knowledge is not what makes you an expert. It is what you do once you gain that knowledge. What will set you apart as an expert is how you explore the realm of the unknown after you have mastered all else.

There is a difference between a person who wants to be an undisputed game-changing expert and someone who is content with mere proficiency. Mastery of current knowledge is the path that leads to expertise; however, it is your exploration of the unknown that distinguishes you. Once you have pushed through the available information, stood on the edge of knowledge, and then pressed further, you become an expert.

Confucius put it this way: "Real knowledge is to know the extent of one's ignorance." What makes you an expert is not your mastery of what is known, but your exploration of what is not known. Great experts are never content with what they already know.

37

ANECDOTE:
MASTER OF KNOWLEDGE

Henry Eyring was a noteworthy chemist and professor at Princeton University in the 1930s and 1940s. He was named a member of the National Science Board by President John F. Kennedy. He served as president of the American Chemical Society and the American Association for the Advancement of Science. In 1967 President Lyndon B. Johnson presented him with the National Medal of Science.

At Princeton, Eyring was a colleague of Albert Einstein, who was by that time known throughout the world. The two men were on friendly terms and spent time together.

According to colleagues and Eyring's biography, on one occasion he walked with Einstein through what had been a rose garden but was then planted with a field crop. Eyring plucked a sprig and asked Einstein if he could identify the type of plant. Einstein looked at the small leaves and responded that he did not know what plant it was. They walked further and found a gardener. When the gardener was asked, he responded that it was soybeans. Thereafter, Eyring was happy to point out, with levity, that Professor Albert Einstein "didn't know beans."[30]

Eyring didn't need to poke fun at Einstein to elevate his own stature. He was, by all accounts, kind and well accomplished. But finding a vulnerability in one of the world's great thinkers was simply too fun to leave alone. He mentioned that experience repeatedly.

Eventually, someone will suggest that you, the expert, don't know beans. If you practice in your specialty long enough, you will meet a nemesis who will find your faults. When this happens, remember Einstein. Take confidence in your knowledge and skill. Some of the greatest experts in history didn't know beans. You are in good company.

38

EXPERT IN PERFORMANCE

Delivering a high-quality body of work that is hard to replicate is the second true mark of an expert. Sometimes your expertise is the consequence of your knowledge, but often it is the result of unmatched execution. You are an expert because you can do things that other people cannot do, or you can perform at a level of proficiency that other people cannot match.

The doing often distinguishes the expert much more than the knowing. There are, of course, some professions where knowledge is the primary measurement of expertise, such as for college professors and politicians. All experts must have knowledge, but for most experts, knowledge is not enough. It is the quality of execution that is paramount.

An orthopedic surgeon I once interviewed was happy when his practice finally hired a new surgeon. After months of searching, the medical group found a qualified young doctor who they thought could perform the procedures required at the large, busy medical practice. Shortly after the new surgeon started, however, it became clear that he did not measure up ability-wise to the expectations of the other surgeons or patients. Eventually, the new surgeon was let go and the group started another lengthy search.

Great experts don't just have knowledge about their field; they also have the ability to deliver a high-quality body of work independent of assistance. This applies to surgeons, engineers, and any other SME. Great experts look for ways to translate their expert knowledge into expert performance. They look for ways to distinguish themselves through the things they do, rather than the things they say.

39

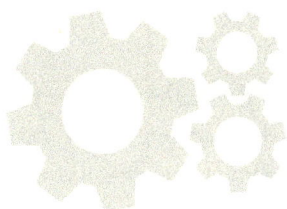

EXPERTS ARE AUTONOMOUS

In the 1980s and 1990s, Carnegie Mellon University in Pittsburgh, Pennsylvania, was a hotbed of research on self-driving vehicles. Computer science and engineering professors and students competed every semester to create the most reliable self-driving technology. The campus quad was set up with a test track for miniature vehicles that drove themselves without real-time operators.

When I graduated from Carnegie Mellon in 1995, it was clear that fully autonomous vehicles had a long way to go. Nothing worthy of consumer adoption was imminent, and critics doubted that fully self-driving vehicles would be possible in their lifetime.

In the decades since, some of the finest scientists in the world have continued to work on creating groundbreaking transportation systems. Eventually, automotive manufacturers deployed advanced driver assistance systems such as anti-lock brakes, adaptive cruise control, lane departure warnings, and automatic steering. These systems were designed to reduce human error, but they were not capable of controlling the vehicle without a licensed human operator.

Automotive experts have debated the merits of driver assistance technologies versus driver replacement technologies for a long time. Driver assistance is incremental and has been deployed broadly in various forms for decades. Driver replacement, on the other hand, has been slow in coming and difficult to achieve.

While there is uncertainty about the pace and breadth of autonomous vehicle adoption, some aspects of this transportation debate are no longer in question. Foremost is that fully autonomous self-driving vehicles are the brass ring that all vehicle manufacturers are pursuing. Full autonomy is the ideal objective and must be attained. Nothing short of it is sufficient. No matter how good driver assistance technology becomes, it must eventually make the driver completely superfluous. Autonomous vehicles are the ultimate objective.

Experts, like self-driving cars, must learn to act alone. They must take responsibility for their own actions and go beyond existing standards. They must be able to handle any problem and any situation without the need for outside direction. Autonomous experts must go beyond their own capabilities and even compensate for the failings of others. They must see things the non-experts do not and accommodate for those things without direction. The ability to operate with full autonomy is an essential trait of any SME, regardless of industry, discipline, or circumstance.

40

EXPERTS MANAGE COMPLEXITY

On January 28, 1986, the space shuttle *Challenger* exploded seventy-three seconds into its flight, killing all seven people on board. It was a major setback for NASA and the Space Shuttle program. In the months that followed, NASA underwent a full investigation by the Rogers Commission.

Among the scientists who studied the shuttle disaster was Richard Feynman, a theoretical physicist and winner of the 1965 Nobel Prize for Physics. Feynman was a vocal critic of NASA, and he was not swayed by politics or public pressure.

During the Rogers Commission's inquiries, NASA officials denied that faulty gaskets and a below-freezing launch temperature caused the disaster. Feynman, however, disagreed. During a public hearing, Feynman took a small piece of the gasket material, crimped it with a small clamp, and deposited the clamp in ice water. In front of NASA officials and multiple news reporters, he explained, "I took the stuff that I got out of your seal and I put it in ice water, and I discovered that when you put some pressure on it for a while and then undo it, [the material] doesn't stretch back, it stays the same dimension. . . . I believe that has some significance for our problem."[31]

Feynman cut through the complexities of NASA and showed, in a very simple way, that sub-freezing temperatures degraded the gaskets used in the shuttle. His demonstration was played repeatedly on national news programs and has been cited countless times by experts in many fields. At a time of high complexity and uncertainty, Feynman brought simplicity and clarity in a way that no one else had.

Richard Branson, the British entrepreneur, investor, and founder of the Virgin Group, said it this way, "Complexity is your enemy. Any fool can make something complicated. It is hard to keep things simple."[32] The Dreyfus and Dreyfus model of skill acquisition suggests that people are not experts, or at least they are not the best experts, until they can effectively manage the complexity of their field of expertise.

All human progress can be summarized as a process of bringing order out of chaos. The best experts are masters of order, masters of clarity, and masters of simplicity.

41

EXPERTS UNDERSTAND CONTEXT

In the Introduction, I mentioned a meeting I attended many years ago at Ford Motor Company. I was participating in a major software development initiative. Despite my intimate knowledge of the project's technology, resources, budgets, and schedules, I was ill-equipped to answer executive-level questions about the strategic effort. My failing, at that time, was not understanding context. I should have known how my project fit into Ford's global strategy and how adjacent initiatives were affected by my work, but I did not.

After decades of personal observation, it is my opinion that this type of error—a lack of understanding of context—is the most common weakness among technical experts. Some of the most capable and competent experts I have met in my career have lacked the ability to understand how their efforts fit into a larger context. They know intimate details about the tools and technologies of their trade, but they know frightfully little about what many of their colleagues do or how they do it.

If experts do not understand the context of their actions, then they will not know how their efforts affect colleagues or customers. They will not know how to make the right decisions for their organization if they do not fully understand the organization's needs. Instead, they will make decisions for themselves and their own myopic domain and will risk imposing disastrous consequences on the people around them.

When SMEs understand context, they know how their expertise intersects with all adjacent SMEs. In my experience at Ford Motor Company, I should have understood how my project affected all interested parties. I knew the facts of my project but not the terrain or processes surrounding it.

The importance of context cannot be overstated. It is the last and highest skill of the Dreyfus and Dreyfus model. It is the skill that differentiates professionals. If your colleagues do not think you fully understand context, then your recommendations will be second-guessed or completely ignored.

I have had the good fortune to work on many software development initiatives with offshore programmers. Without exception, context is the most frequently missing ingredient of the offshore resources. Software developers on another continent, in another culture, working for another company, often speaking another language, struggle to master context. They miss things that local technicians quickly catch, and they assume things that local technicians don't. In fairness, offshore developers have a monumental task. It is almost an impossible expectation for them to maintain consistent mastery of context. Few people can accomplish it.

Finally, context is a major source of confusion and frustration for less experienced technical professionals. They know their technology singularly well, but they misunderstand or dismiss the perspectives of others. Mastery of context is the difference between promotion and stagnation, credibility and rejection, respect and denial.

42

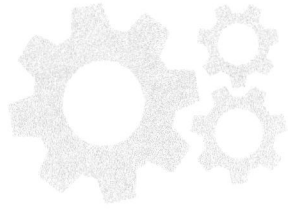

EXPERTISE AS A
PROFESSIONAL ROLE

*"I argue that expertise and its development are not
primarily dependent upon knowledge and skills in
cognitive structure, but on embodied being in the world,
inescapably entwined with others and things."*

—Gloria Dall'Alba, Associate Professor, School of Education,
University of Queensland, Australia[33]

In a professional setting, expertise is a social agreement and a mechanism for efficient management of knowledge. All people in an organization cannot possess all relevant knowledge at all times; therefore, knowledge is consolidated by domain. The custodians of that consolidated knowledge are often regarded by their organizations as subject matter experts.

Several interdependencies can be found between SMEs and the laypeople who interact with them. If any of these interdependencies are absent from the relationship, the role of the SME is diminished or eliminated.

Researchers Harald Mieg and Julia Evetts summarized the link between experts and laypeople with a diagram similar to the following:[34]

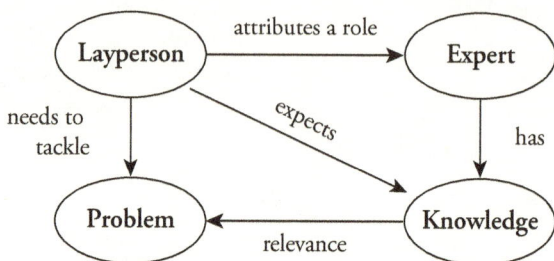

First, laypeople must have a problem that they cannot satisfy alone. Without problems that require the concentration of knowledge, there is no need for expertise. As discussed previously, it does not matter if the expert claims superior status; it only matters if laypeople grant the expert that status. Without that, the expert has no unique influence. Second, laypeople expect the expert to have knowledge sufficient to solve the problem. If the expert does not possess the knowledge, either because the expert has not obtained it or because the knowledge does not yet exist, then the model breaks down. All interdependencies must be present or none of the benefits of expertise and expert performance are realized.

It is also important to note that interdependencies are constantly in motion. Laypeople have ever-changing needs and expectations. Similarly, the expert's knowledge and competency are always advancing or declining. Consequently, laypeople are constantly changing the perceived value of expert roles.

SMEs must remain relevant, and they can do this by staying well ahead of any layperson's constantly improving competency and by maintaining knowledge and skills adequate enough for the problems laypeople need to resolve.

43

INNATE TALENT

A debate over nature versus nurture rages regarding expertise, just as it does in many other sciences. Are experts the product of genetics, training, or both? Can anyone become an expert, regardless of genetic composition? Are the prodigies and savants destined at birth to become top performers? Research on this topic varies.

Sir Francis Galton was a cousin of Charles Darwin. He invented modern statistical regression and standard deviation. He also formulated many of the current philosophies about fingerprinting and intelligence testing. He was, by any reasonable measure, an intelligent person.

One of Galton's published works was the book *Hereditary Genius*. In it, Galton indicated that eminent individuals in society are generally the descendants of a small group of people. Humans, he concluded, have an inherited potential that determines their prospects for exceptional accomplishments. If a person's physical stature is influenced by genetics, then so too must be the size of one's brain, mental capacity, and generic competence.

Galton's work was the beginning of a philosophy that continued in scholarship for a century. Certain people, it was thought, are genetically endowed with superior traits. Galton coined the term *eugenics* in 1883 to promote the idea that the human species could be improved through reproductive manipulation. His work would eventually be used as support for selective mating, forced sterilization, and genocide. Galton's thinking influenced Adolf Hitler and many others of similar ilk.[35]

Decades later, many of Galton's hypotheses were rejected and relegated to the intellectual trash heap. Some of his thinking about genetics, however, survives today. There is a notion, for example, fostered by Galton and perpetuated in Western thought that certain people are born with superior endowments. We speak of these people as "prodigies," "unexplained geniuses," "wonder children," or "talent freaks of nature." It turns out, however, that researchers have found no verifiable evidence supporting Galton's idea of general superiority. No one, it turns out, is born to succeed or dominate.[36]

Anders Ericsson, who we mentioned previously regarding the 10,000-hour rule, was one of the most accomplished researchers in the field of expertise and expert performance in modern times. He passed away in 2020,[37] and it has been said of him that "no one [else] has had a greater impact on scientific and popular views of expertise."[38] Ericsson studied and wrote about the subject for decades. He believed that genetics have very little to do with expertise. Rather, he posited that training is what distinguishes top performers from the rest of the pack. In his book *Peak: Secrets from the New Science of Expertise*, he wrote, "The bottom line is that every time you look closely . . . you find that the extraordinary abilities are the product of much practice and training. Prodigies and savants don't give us any reason to believe that some people are born with natural abilities in one field or another."[39] Ericsson, and many like him, discounted the influence of genetics.

In 2018, researchers Joseph Baker and Nick Wattie concluded that innate talent is "necessary but not sufficient to explain exceptional performance."[40] Also that year, researcher Robert Plomin put it this way: "There is no simple answer to the question of what it takes to become an expert. It's not just training, and it's not just talent. Training without talent will not take you to the top tiers of expertise, nor will talent without training. It's not just nature, and it's not just nurture; experts are born and made."[41] The trophy goes to the committed, the patient, the dogged, and the persistent. The smartest people are not necessarily and indeed rarely are the best experts.

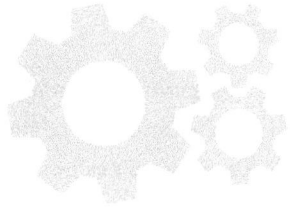

44

EXPERTS ARE THREE-DIMENSIONAL

Too many experts believe that their impact is determined by their level of proficiency in their field. They equate their effectiveness to their degree of know-how or technical skill. They believe they are experts because they are good at what they do, they have more knowledge than others, and they are better educated, with more degrees or years of study. They also believe they have better credentials and deliver better results than others. These are important aspects of being an expert, but they are incomplete.

All experts, regardless of industry, discipline, country, or culture, will influence others using these three things:

1. Knowledge

2. Skill

3. Attitude

Unfortunately, many experts see themselves on just one of these planes. They achieve success in one dimension and cling to it ever after. Some experts even dismiss the other two dimensions as irrelevant or unimportant. The expert scientist, for example, may see little value in developing an amiable personality, while the expert musician, on the other hand, may find little use for the mathematics that underpins all music. Because of their narrow perspective, both will remain limited in their influence and power.

For experts to maximize their impact, they must be more than just sages of knowledge or highly skilled at what they do. Experts who wield influence, who make a difference, and who cause change engage all three dimensions.

45

ANECDOTE: THREE DIMENSIONS

My younger brother, Ryan, is a wonderful man. He has worked as a paramedic in Atlanta, Georgia, for more than twenty-five years. His lengthy service has refined his ability to assess perilous situations and determine effective ways to respond. Ryan has developed these skills through vigilance and repetition, which have made his actions nearly automatic. Whether a person is shot, stabbed, or hit by a vehicle, Ryan possesses the skills to act in life-saving ways with confidence and immediacy.

Ryan is also a fount of knowledge regarding his profession. He has studied and practiced his craft with enough discipline to identify the truth in crisis situations quickly and accurately. He knows how to diagnose life-threatening ailments and how to use the medical tools at his disposal to aid his patients.

In addition to his skill and knowledge, there is something more. Ryan's presence, all six feet, two inches and three hundred pounds of it, is reassuring and comforting. Despite his imposing stature, he is kind, patient, and gentle. People are likely to feel safer and calmer by the mere look on his countenance. If an accident or illness befalls you in Atlanta, heaven forbid, you want my brother to be the one to help.

Researchers and scholars who study expertise typically write about the subject as a combination of skill and knowledge. In recent years, however, researchers, like Gloria Dall'Alba, a professor at the University of Queensland in Australia, have been looking more closely at the third ingredient: attitude. Dall'Alba has observed that expertise appears to "incorporate not only high levels of knowledge and skills, but also something else besides." She concludes that expertise is a combination of knowledge, skill, and an "embodied being in the world, inescapably entwined with others and things."[42]

Developing expertise must include ways of performing tasks with proficiency and skill. It also includes mastering the subject and knowing the truths that govern the domain. And, finally, expertise is a form of being. It is the manner of interaction between oneself and the world. It is the edge of contact. It is the way Ryan interacts with patients, beyond his skill and his knowledge.

In short, scholars point to three dimensions that make up an expert. Similarly, so do my professional observations. Expertise is the skillful way of doing things, the truth that governs its domain, and the life that draws people to it.

46

MASLOW'S HIERARCHY OF NEEDS

Becoming an expert is not just a worthy personal objective. It is more than a path toward higher income or higher social status. Expertise, if we are to believe psychologist Abraham Maslow's theory of human motivation, is a fundamental human need. It is a motivating force of nature that is manifest in all people. Just as breathing, drinking, and eating are physiological needs for human survival, expertise and expert performance are self-actualizing emotional needs that are hardwired into the human psyche. Maslow stated it this way: "What a man can be, he must be."

Just as people need food to eat and water to drink, just as they need safety and social standing, and just as they need esteem, recognition, and status, they need expertise. Self-actualization, according to Maslow, is the most intense human need and one of the highest we experience on the hierarchy of needs.

Some people have a strong desire to excel in athletics, others in the arts, and others in academia. All, however, are motivated by a need to reach their full potential. This is more than a desire; it is, according to Maslow, an inherent human need.[43]

47

EXPERTS EMPLOY DELIBERATE PRACTICE

Psychology professor Anders Ericsson spent his lengthy career studying people who excel in their fields and the processes by which they achieve peak performance. After decades of research and thousands of interviews, Ericsson determined that top performance in almost any field requires practice. A lot of practice. But he also determined that experts don't just practice a lot, they practice differently. They don't just engage in rigorous or highly specific practice. No, top performers employ what Ericsson called "deliberate practice."

According to Ericsson, deliberate practice contains seven common traits:[44]

1. *Stand on shoulders.* Top performers learn all they can from people who have gone before them. They don't waste time reinventing past innovations. They seek coaches and mentors who have the most experience and learn as much as possible from them.

2. *Go beyond comfort.* The best experts don't stop practicing when they become proficient. They push the boundaries of their proficiency and capability. They exercise to the point of exhaustion, physically, mentally, and emotionally.

3. *Set specific goals.* Experts don't just practice randomly. They are specific about what skills they are deficient in, what needs to be improved, and exactly how they can make changes.

4. *Full attention.* Deliberate practice begins when your mind is fully engaged, and it ends when your mind starts to wander. To practice with full concentration is far more effective than practicing while daydreaming. Practicing while daydreaming is essentially a waste of time.

5. *Feedback.* People cannot improve if they don't collect direct feedback and employ the means for modifying behavior based on that feedback.

6. *Mental model.* Great performers know what great performance looks like. They have seen it in others, or they have had leaders help them create the mental model. They know what kind of performance they want.

7. *Modify skills.* Improvements in performance are almost always based on the layering of skills on top of previously acquired skills.

Of course, all seven traits of deliberate practice may not always be possible. Coaches or mentors can be scarce, for example. But research has shown that the more closely an expert follows the principles of deliberate practice, the better. Deliberate practice is faster and more reliable at creating expert performance than any known alternative.

48

STUDY THE COMPETITION

When a new car is released from Lexus, BMW, Mercedes, or Cadillac, the first customer in line to buy is an employee from Ford Motor Company. The car is ordered incognito and picked up immediately when available. It is taken to a Ford test track and multiple laboratories. It is driven hard and every system, subsystem, and component level are evaluated. Eventually, the vehicle is disassembled. Every weld is torn apart, every screw loosened, and every drop of glue dissolved. Within three months, hundreds of engineers will reduce the new car to a pile of parts and fragments in a nondescript test facility. Ford will glean as much information as possible from their competitors' products, and it will systematically catalog every bit of knowledge it extracts. Few industries are as comprehensive at competitive analysis as the automotive industry.

Likewise, great SMEs study their competitors. They know the alternatives to their own solutions. They identify who serves their market and what products, pricing, distribution, and promotions are employed. They know their competitors' strengths and weaknesses. And they know their competitors' people.

Competitive knowledge helps an SME in many ways, but here are two of the most important. First, knowing your competitor's strengths will teach you how to improve your own goods and services. If a competitor's product is better than yours in an important dimension, then that dimension is a prospective area for improvement. Great SMEs study their competition so they can identify, refine, and focus on their own progress.

Second, competitors' weaknesses are the keys to winning against them in the marketplace. The SME who has details about an opponent's weaknesses knows how to defeat them. As a result, SMEs have greater influence in their organization and in the eyes of their customers, because they know how to improve, they know how to compete, and they know how to win.

DON'T PRAISE COMPETITORS

Don't praise the competition. You should respect it and appreciate it, but praise it? No, absolutely not. Not once. Not ever!

Nothing good comes to a company if its SMEs heap admiration on the competition. Don't do it yourself and don't support it from your colleagues. No matter how stellar your competitors may be, they don't deserve your praise. Praise is reserved for the people on your team.

Some SMEs have the mistaken notion that speaking supportively about the opposing team will make them sound informed and objective. They think that their unsolicited praise of the competition will make them appear unbiased and trustworthy. To the contrary, praising the competition makes the SME look disloyal and weak. You do a tremendous disservice to your reputation, your company, and your cause when you praise your competitors.

If the SME offers one awkward word of praise for a competitor followed by a thousand persuasive words about their own services, the competitor wins, and handsomely. If your competitor can capture your compliment, even if taken out of context, they will weaponize it and play it to your customers repeatedly.

Of course, SMEs must have in-depth knowledge of the competitive landscape. They should know the strengths and weaknesses of each product on the market. But they must not gather competitive knowledge just to give it away to any prospective customer who asks a probing question.

If it can be avoided, an SME should never mention a competitor by name. If asked directly about a competitor, the SME should skirt the question and talk about their own product or service. Questions about the competition should never be used as an opportunity to compliment them, nor should they be used as a reason for negativity. Just because the SME knows a lot about the competition doesn't mean a question should pry open the floodgates. If pressed, and only if pressed, the SME can provide a direct one-sentence negative review of the competitor that hits at the heart of the competitor's most vulnerable weakness. The SME should always bring into focus their strengths and their competitor's weaknesses—never the other way around.

Never praise competitors.

50

BE LIKABLE

In 2008 the US Democratic Party brought the presidential primary race to New Hampshire. A debate was held between four candidates including then-Senators Hillary Clinton and Barack Obama. During the event, the moderator directed a question at Clinton: "You are the most experienced and the most electable. . . . But what can you say to the voters of New Hampshire who see your resume and like it, but are hesitating on the likability issue? They seem to like Barack Obama more?"

To this, Clinton responded, "Well, that hurts my feelings." She then paused, played to the pity of her audience by dropping her head, and said, "But I'll try to go on."

In acquiescence, she added, "He's very likable. I agree with that. I don't think I'm that bad."

Obama then paid her the unforgettable backhanded compliment of the entire campaign: "You're likable enough, Hillary."[45]

During that debate, Clinton was the expert. And eight years later when she ran again and debated Donald Trump, she was the expert again. But both times she lost the election. Just because experts have talent, education, and experience, it does not mean people will like them. In fact, the more accomplished an expert becomes, the higher the probability that likability will be an issue.

Of course, there are many times when expertise is more important than temperament, but temperament matters, and it matters a lot more than some experts think. Likable people gain trust and influence. If your audience likes you, they will overlook your flaws, as well as flaws in your product or service. They will forgive and forget old issues. They will award you with more business and will pay you more money. If something goes wrong, and it eventually will, people who like you will give you the benefit of the doubt and minimize the error. Being likable has many advantages.

Most experts understand that they should try to be likable, yet many do little to address deficiencies in this area. Let's face it, for some experts, being likable is difficult, and in fact some of them became experts intentionally so they could justify their unlikability. For them it is easier to become an expert in their field of study than to develop a pleasant personality. Some experts would never allow themselves to have a knowledge gap in their field of expertise, yet they will spend their entire careers with likability gaps in their personality.

Your competition is working hard at being likable even if you are not. Most non-experts know that if they cannot outsmart an expert then they still have a good chance of beating that person by being more amiable, more pleasant, more appealing, and more good-natured.

As hard as it may seem for some experts, they can learn to be likable. This is not about just being tolerable, by the way. Many experts are tolerable, but few are truly charming. Likable experts acknowledge other people and are kind, pleasant, and friendly. If those things don't come naturally, then an expert should practice until they can genuinely have those qualities in their interactions with other people. Showing genuine interest in an audience and listening to them when they speak will take an expert a long way.

In addition, being likable means being sympathetic and patient. It means realizing that people are more important than expertise. Being likable means remaining happy even when it is hard to be happy and refraining from easily becoming irritable or angry. Likable people are not disagreeable, even when they disagree.

Great experts take the time to discover things about their audience that is sincerely interesting and laudable. They do thoughtful and kind things for their audience or, better yet, for their audiences' colleagues. One of the most likable things any person can do is to help another person's child. Find ways to help people and lift them. If you are an expert and you are likable, truly likable, then you cannot be stopped. Likability and industry-leading expertise are a rare combination.

Experts should never be satisfied with being "likeable enough." If someone says you are likable enough, then be assured, you are *not* likable enough. If Senator Clinton did not prove that likability is essential in 2008, then she certainly did in 2016.

51

EXPERTS RECOGNIZE THEIR OWN FAILINGS

Years ago, a young engineer went to Australia on vacation. While there, he purchased a souvenir boomerang. It was carved from wood and painted with an Aboriginal design. He knew his colleagues who were mechanical engineers would appreciate the design, style, and function of the simple object.

When he returned to work, as expected, the unique object captured the curiosity of many of his coworkers. What was it about the object's shape that made it fly as it did?

Over lunch, the engineers discussed the properties of the boomerang—the essential curves, the lift, the angles, the rotation, the balance points, the velocities, and more. They decided that the cheap souvenir contained many design flaws that would limit its effectiveness. Eventually, they decided to design the perfect boomerang.

As a side project, an office hobby of sorts, the team designed a flawless boomerang. They collaborated through computer-aided design (CAD) software. They calculated the perfect shape, the perfect dimensions, and the perfect mass. They even ran their design through a simulated wind tunnel to prove its effectiveness. In short order, they concluded that they had perfected their boomerang design. Even when it was thrown poorly, they believed their boomerang would return to its starting place.

Finally, the engineers decided it was time to prove their mechanical prowess. They retrieved a piece of plexiglass from the company's shop and loaded it into a lathe. They sent their CAD design to the lathe that cut and polished the plastic into a shape they believed to be the perfect boomerang.

The team was proud of their product and anxious to test their work. The small group went to a nearby grassy field, followed by about thirty of their colleagues. Surrounded by his peers, the lead engineer took the boomerang, held it at the best angle, and launched it with full force out over the field.

Immediately the entire group of engineers and spectators discovered a major defect in the otherwise perfectly designed boomerang: It was created from completely clear plastic. Now flying in a circular path, the boomerang had vanished from sight. No one could see it at all! There was not even the slightest blur in the clear sky. In an instant, everyone let out a collective gasp. While the engineers did not know where the boomerang was, they did know exactly where it was headed. Within seconds, the spectators panicked and started running toward the building. Others crouched on the ground. Everyone anticipated that someone would be struck, and it was impossible to know who or when. Fortunately, the boomerang flew in a circular path and landed safely in the grass a few feet from where it was thrown.

The boomerang engineers are not alone in their blunder. The list of colossal failures like theirs is long and growing. There is no end to the massive public failures we've seen among SMEs. Airport security on 9/11 failed. The experts who designed and launched the space shuttles *Challenger* and *Columbia* failed. The engineers who designed the I-35 bridge in Minnesota that collapsed failed. The American and European national security agencies who declared that Iraq had weapons of mass destruction failed. Bankers and regulators who oversaw the mortgage industry in the mid-2000s failed. Enron executives failed. The designers of British Petroleum's Deepwater Horizon platform failed. The engineers who designed the levees in New Orleans failed. The list could go on and on.

As an expert, you will fail. It is inevitable. Consequently, great experts anticipate failure, face it head on, and do everything they can to mitigate the consequences of such failure in their work.

52

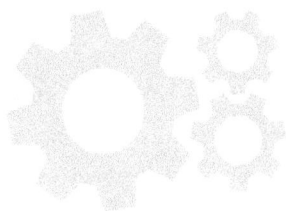

FOR GOOD OR ILL

We need experts for almost everything. We need expert programmers, engineers, doctors, lawyers, writers, mechanics, and teachers. In many cases, our lives depend on experts who can perform tasks that we cannot perform for ourselves. When we experience a sharp pain in our chest, for example, many of us will place ourselves in the hands of a cardiologist, an expert. Even when we don't absolutely need experts, we seek them anyway. We watch expert athletes, actors, musicians, and comedians. We willingly pay a premium for expertise. When our children go to college, we encourage them to focus on a highly specialized field and become experts. We spend hundreds of thousands or millions of dollars training and tutoring people of all ages to become experts. The primary source of social and economic progress in the world is the expert. Medical and nutrition experts have created improved health and longevity worldwide. Transportation experts enable people to travel with speed, comfort, and safety. Technology experts have enabled instant communications. SMEs are the primary reason that humans no longer die young on farms, in huts, lit only by candlesticks. However, as important and influential as experts are, not all of them are worthy of praise.

SMEs have brought us some of the worst catastrophes and toughest challenges in human history, like the slave trade and the Holocaust. Take, for example, Trofim Lysenko, a Ukrainian agricultural expert from the Stalin era. In the 1950s, the Chinese government chose to follow his dogma regarding agricultural practices. Immediately, food production in China dropped dramatically. Between 1958 and 1962, as many as thirty-six million Chinese citizens starved to death.[46]

On April 26, 1986, Anatoly Stepanovich Dyatlov was the deputy chief engineer at the Chernobyl Nuclear Power Plant. Contrary to the advice of at least two subordinates, he ordered the continuation of an ill-fated nuclear experiment that melted down a reactor. His actions caused the death of thousands of people, the forced relocation of 350,000 citizens, and the contamination of five million residences.[47]

Aimé Le Médec was the captain of the SS *Mont-Blanc*, a cargo vessel. On December 6, 1917, the ship was fully loaded with explosives in route to France. While entering Halifax harbor in Nova Scotia, Canada, the ship collided with another vessel. The resulting blast was the largest man-made explosion to that date in history. An eleven-hundred-pound section of the ship's anchor was thrown over two miles away. Two thousand people were killed and nearly ten thousand injured. Twelve thousand buildings were destroyed in the blast.[48]

Angelo Mozilo was the CEO of Countrywide Financial at the epicenter of the financial industry's subprime mortgage crisis. As cofounder of Countrywide, he engaged in aggressive lending practices and derivative selling. The company grew to become the largest mortgage lender in America and then its largest financial disaster. In 2010 he agreed to pay a settlement and receive an industry ban rather than go to trial.

Expertise, it turns out, has a way of exposing the best and the worst of human thought and ingenuity. With virtue, expertise can be a blessing to the entire human family. Used with malice or recklessness, however, expertise can be a curse.

ESTABLISH TRUST

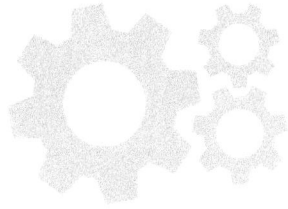

53

THE FOUNDATION
OF TRUST

As mentioned earlier, when a corporate SME meets with customers, they have three primary responsibilities: establish trust, determine mutual vision, and ensure delivery. Everything else is secondary. We'll talk about vision and delivery later in this book. For now, let's focus on trust.

The most important asset an expert can obtain is trust. It is more important than technical prowess or an industry-changing idea. When people trust you—when you win their faith, confidence, and admiration, they seek your advice, they value your opinion, and they do what you recommend.

Trust is forward-looking. It is based on a person's confidence or faith in some future event or condition. When people trust you, they believe that you can shape their future for the better. It also means they will submit some level of control in their life to you. Being worthy of trust is one of your highest objectives. You may be an expert in all dimensions, but if you do not have the trust of your audience, then you have nothing.

54

SMES, SALES, AND TRUST

We see it repeatedly in companies throughout the world. A sales representative identifies a large prospective customer and initiates pursuit. They fly to meetings and represent the company with carefully crafted product information. They qualify the customer's needs, ascertain the budget, and begin navigating the customer's decision-making hierarchy. They establish relationships with product users, purchasing influencers, executive sponsors, and others. They filter members of the organization to eliminate points of friction or dissent. Eventually, they assemble a compelling proposal or recommendation and makes a pitch.

At some point in this process, if the customer is serious about buying, a stream of questions begins to flow in the sales representative's direction. The prospective customer asks about product capability, customizations, compatibility, scale, service levels, security, safety, and so on—more questions than the sales representative can answer alone. So, to strengthen the proposal and their company's chances at securing a deal, the sales representative obtains support from their organization. A subject matter expert is assigned to help. Sometimes, if the deal is large enough, an entire team of SMEs is assembled. Complex products are almost always sold with SMEs participating in the deal.

When an SME participates in the selling process, things quickly get complicated. The sales representative, who has forged relationships for weeks, months, or even years, is now involving other people who will either help push the opportunity across the finish line or obliterate all chances of doing so. The SME could end up being either a blessing or a curse. And, as important as the SME may be to the deal, few SMEs are adequately trained in the sales craft.

Most SMEs, for example, believe that they are involved in the selling process to answer the prospective customer's questions. Given the scenario I just described, why else would they be involved? As I mentioned, there are questions the sales representative cannot answer adequately and that is why the SME is engaged. That's the typical process. But there is a big difference between *when* an SME becomes involved and *why* an SME becomes involved. The SME becomes involved *when* questions from the customer warrant it, but the SME is involved *because* they are needed to establish or maintain trust. The questions are the *when*; building trust (not just answering questions) is the *why*.

Questions reveal the customer's sources of distrust in you, the sales representative, other members of your team, your product, or your organization. Therefore, great SMEs use those questions to target trust. Of course, the customer's questions must be answered, but that is the easy part. You can answer questions perfectly yet fail to build trust. The difficult task, and the most important one, is the process of building a trusting relationship. That is *why* the SME is involved. Yes, SMEs should answer questions, but their purpose, first and foremost, should be to build trust, because it is foundational.

In this section we examine some of the key principles of establishing and maintaining trust with the goal to increase SME confidence with clients, decrease misunderstandings, and eliminate common gaffs. Let's get going.

55

EARLY EVIDENCE OF TRUSTING EXPERTS

Reliance on experts for making important decisions is an age-old practice. Nearly twenty-five hundred years ago, Socrates recorded:

> I observe that when a decision has to be taken at the state assembly about some matter of building, they send for the builders to give their advice about the buildings, and when it concerns shipbuilding, they send for the shipwrights, and similarly in every case where they are dealing with a subject which they think can be learned and taught. But if anyone else tries to give advice, who they don't regard as an expert, no matter how handsome or wealthy or well-born he is, they still will have none of him, but jeer at him and create an uproar, until either the would-be speaker is shouted down and gives up of his own accord, or else the police drag him away or put him out on the order of the presidents.[49]

56

TYPES OF TRUST

There are many types of trust, but SMEs should be particularly attuned to two types that are universally important. First, people must be able to trust your skills or capabilities, and second, people must be able to trust your motives.

Trust starts with competence. If your audience does not have reason to believe you are capable of performing the desired tasks, then they will not trust you. When people trust your skills, they believe that you have the technical competence to perform a task and obtain a desired outcome. They believe you can accomplish something that they cannot do on their own.

When someone trusts your motives, they believe that you will care for their interests above your own. When someone fully trusts you as an expert, they will give you power, in the hope that you will accomplish a desired outcome, even if that outcome runs contrary to your own desired outcome.

Typically, we trust people who have excellent skills and who do not have ulterior motives. If people do not trust you as an expert, they will not follow you or give you power. It's that simple. Either they do not trust that you can produce the desired outcome, or they do not believe that your advice is in their best interest. They either do not trust your skills or they do not trust your motive.

TRUST IN SKILLS

To be trusted, SMEs must deliver superior results on a consistent basis. If they do, then they may be trusted, and they do not, then they won't be trusted. Competence is an essential prerequisite to trust, but it is certainly not sufficient to guarantee trust.

If SMEs are not capable of delivering what is expected, then they are left with three options:

1. They can improve their skills and knowledge to consistently deliver services above the level expected. This is the ideal. Producing results that surpass expectations and continuously improve is always preferred. This is the only reliable path for any person to obtain and maintain performance-based trust. No SME should be satisfied with their performance while failure is a possibility, no matter how remote that possibility may be.

2. They can reset unrealistic customer expectations in an honest fashion. SMEs will not be successful if the customer's hopes are irrational or baseless. Resetting expectations is an essential skill, especially for experts who are routinely asked to be miracle workers. SMEs should help customers and colleagues see the future as it really will be. Not setting realistic expectations virtually assures disappointment or failure.

3. They can opt to knowingly under-deliver. As untenable as this approach may seem in some disciplines, it is rational and justified by some experts. The software industry, for example, is filled with experts who have consistently failed to predict timing and resource requirements for software development projects. For decades software experts have failed at forecasting. Their redemption has only been through the utterly abysmal failures of other software experts by comparison. Knowingly under-delivering may be acceptable in some select fields, but it is not a recipe for sustained success, even in software development.

Ideally, experts should provide clear justification for the trust that is granted to them. They should prove, empirically, that they are sufficient for the task at hand and that they will consistently over-deliver. Actor Julie Andrews of *The Sound of Music* fame, is credited as saying, "An amateur rehearses until he gets it right. A professional rehearses until he can't get it wrong."

58

TRUST IS AN EMOTION

Trust is an emotion. And like other emotions, it can be messy and complicated. Psychologist Robert Plutchik has said that trust is one of our eight primary emotions. (The other seven are anger, fear, sadness, surprise, anticipation, joy, and disgust.) According to Plutchik, trust is correlated with acceptance, admiration, submission, joy, and love. Trusted experts who consistently bring joy into the lives of the people they serve will eventually be loved by them. Similarly, experts who consistently bring joy without an ulterior motive into the lives of the people they serve will themselves grow to love those people.

Business relationships are typically maintained on the basis of mutual respect, dignity, and separation—not on love, joy, or submission. But just because emotions are muted in professional settings does not mean that the full gamut of emotional undercurrents are not present. In spite of what appears on the surface, businesses are emotional places. People bring their emotional baggage to the table, most of it negative, and the stress of an occupation heightens and accentuates our emotional condition.

Your goal as an SME is to move all customers and colleagues gently yet decisively into the emotional state of trust. You do that by easing apprehension and eliminating fear. Acceptance is a mild form of trust, just as apprehension is a mild form of fear. Mutual acceptance, therefore, is the starting point for trust. Admiration is trust's most persuasive cousin. Build trust. Seek trust. Demonstrate trust. Abide in trust.

59

TRUST IN MOTIVES

As a young adult, I owned an old car. I knew the car was in bad condition, but I didn't want to pay the high price of replacing it. Eventually, I took the car to a dealership for a repair. A mechanic recommended I replace the vehicle. In response I thought to myself, "Of course he wants me to purchase a new car. Selling me a new car is in his interest."

Without hesitation I rejected the mechanic's recommendation because I assumed his suggestion was self-serving. I assumed he wanted me to buy a new car because he made more money selling new cars than servicing old ones. Of course, years later I learned the opposite is true, that dealerships actually make far more profits repairing old cars than selling new ones. Nevertheless, I made a judgment about his motive and discounted his recommendation based purely upon my perception of his true goal.

Months later the father of a friend looked at my car. I knew that he tinkered with cars as a hobby, he was a generation older than me, and he was confident when he talked about automobiles. He looked under the hood of my car and said, "Alan, it's time to get a new car." I immediately believed him. A week later, I was driving a new vehicle.

Why was it so easy for me to reject the recommendation of a certified mechanic and accept the recommendation of a hobbyist? Of the two the mechanic was certainly more qualified. My actions can only be ascribed to my perception of motive. The words of my friend's father were easy for me to accept because I knew he would not benefit from my actions. My decision to buy a vehicle or repair my old one did not impact him, financially or otherwise.

The mechanic, on the other hand, failed to convince me to purchase a replacement vehicle because I did not trust his motive. He may have been completely trustworthy. In retrospect, he probably was. But I did not know it at the time, and I would not give him the benefit of my trust. I assumed, as most people would, that his recommendation was primarily motivated by his own personal gain.

Herein is one of the key lessons for experts. Your audience will always judge your recommendations based on their assumptions about your motive. If your motive can be interpreted in two ways, it will be interpreted the least favorably. Your audience will not accept your recommendation without considering what you as an expert stand to gain or lose. In fact, they care more about your motive than your knowledge or your skill.

One of the mistakes experts make when offering recommendations is relying exclusively on logic. They assume their audience is rational and will make their decisions based on quantifiable and verifiable facts. Most SMEs don't even acknowledge that their audience is judging their motive. Be clear to people about what you personally stand to gain or lose. Motive matters. It matters a lot. Motive matters first, and motive matters most.

60

RELATIONSHIPS ARE BUILT ON TRUST

Years ago, I was working for a consulting company. The president, Sandy Moore, invited me to a lunch appointment with an executive from one of our largest clients. Sandy knew this executive well; they had worked together for decades.

The lunch conversation was casual. Sandy and the executive discussed golf, college-aged children, and a musical they'd both seen in New York City. I was completely out of my element. I didn't play golf. My children were in diapers, not college. I went to movies, not Broadway musicals. Besides, how was any of that banter germane to the multimillion-dollar relationship between our two companies? Why did Sandy ask me to attend this lunch?

Eventually, in an effort to contribute to the conversation, I abruptly changed the subject and started talking about technology trends, recent projects, and some of the key employees of our consulting firm. Sandy looked at me as if I had said or done something offensive. It was awkward.

I was expected to be an expert, but I floundered in that setting. If the client was not interested in my thoughts about technology, processes, quality, or controls, then how could I make a meaningful impact? I was lost. But Sandy knew something I did not. She knew that trust in a relationship comes before technology. If you do not have the client's trust, then no explanation of system designs, development, or deployment will matter to them. Sandy was interested in establishing a relationship of trust while I was only interested in expounding on technology.

61

THE ASYMMETRY
OF TRUST

Trust is lopsided. In a trusting relationship, one party gives the trust and the other party receives it. It always goes in one direction. Two people may have mutual trust for one another, but this is two instances of trust, not just one. Balanced mutual trust is of course ideal, particularly in relationships where partners are equal, such as a marriage, but even an equal partnership is not a paragon of symmetrical trust. I trust my wife, for instance, to speak fluent Spanish, but she cannot trust me in the same way. We have different skills, different interests, and different motives. Consequently, we trust each other in subtly different and nuanced ways. Trust is as unique as the people who give and receive it.

Because imbalances exist in relationships, asymmetry can be accentuated. Employers and employees, for example, have much different forms of trust in each other. SMEs and laypeople have different knowledge and different skills. Consequently, their trust in each other is much different. A medical patient may have complete trust in a doctor's skills and motivation, but that same doctor may have low confidence that the patient will follow a prescribed treatment regimen. The patient's trust in the doctor is much different than the doctor's trust in the patient.

In addition, trust is granted by the trustor; it can never be compelled by the other party. When trust is violated, it is typically violated in one direction. Trust is hard to gain but easy to lose. The asymmetries abound.

The importance of this imbalance for SMEs is the fact that you may not be trusted as much as you think you are. Just because you feel comfortable and trusted in a relationship does not mean that the other party feels the same way. They may not trust you, and they may not trust your colleagues. SMEs are in positions of power, which means there is a natural imbalance of knowledge and skill. As a result, experts often receive added scrutiny. Don't automatically assume that people trust you. You may be completely trustworthy, but that does not mean you are completely trusted. Always recognize trust as the lopsided, asymmetrical emotion that it is.

62

THE GENETICS
OF TRUST

Genetics influence almost all human attributes. Our genes affect our appearance, our intelligence, and our susceptibility to ailments. Researchers have also determined that our personality is highly influenced by genetics. Some scientists anticipate that nearly all personality traits will eventually be linked to our genetic code. But there is at least one human trait that defies genetics. So far, it appears that our ability to trust is not genetically determined or even genetically influenced.

Infants begin life with a high capacity to trust. They are suspicious of no one. Over time, however, their ability to trust diminishes. They eventually learn that all people have flaws and that many things will cause them harm. Children discover that they are vulnerable creatures. They realize that mistrust and caution are far more likely to ensure security than unthinking trust.

Some people trust experts instantly, while others not at all. Any bestowal of trust is far more a statement of the trustor than the trusted. Of course, there is nothing an expert can do about an audience's history, but SMEs should be aware that a person's ability to trust them was molded through years of experience. An expert's credentials or logic may be enough to gain the trust of some people, but they are probably not enough to gain the trust of everyone. Just because a person does not trust an expert immediately does not mean that person is unintelligent or ill-informed. To the contrary, someone's ability to trust means they have traversed a life of experience and they have been conditioned by their environment to trust or distrust. Often their impulse is a learned response for their own survival.

63

ASSOCIATIONS

The adage, "It ain't what you know, it's who you know," holds special meaning for SMEs. In typical parlance, the saying is used to suggest that someone was hired or promoted because of a relationship rather than because of merit. Often muttered in conjunction with a shrug and a smirk, the saying can be employed as a nonchalant accusation of nepotism, bias, or outright discrimination.

For you as an SME, however, the saying points to something much more important: that everything you say to an audience, no matter how logical or how factual, can be overruled by one well-positioned antagonist. People are more strongly influenced by the people they already know than by any well-intended or well-spoken expert. Old relationships trump new information.

To combat this relationship dilemma, SMEs can add mass to what they say by establishing strong relationships themselves. If many people inside your organization know and trust you, then what you say will carry more weight, not because what you say is more accurate or compelling but because the people you know you will likely support you. Many times, I have seen recommendations from SMEs rejected until a supporting colleague intervened. Sometimes, and maybe far too often, who you know is indeed more important than what you know. So, great SMEs pursue strong professional relationships.

Associations matter. Most of the time they matter very little, but sometimes they matter a lot. Make yourself available to good associations. Take the time to network with people in your field, among your colleagues, and with your customers. Be a mentor to up-and-coming professionals. Be prepared to dissociate from those who detract or degrade. Associate with those who bring credit to your expertise, who value your contribution, and who will support you when others resist.

64

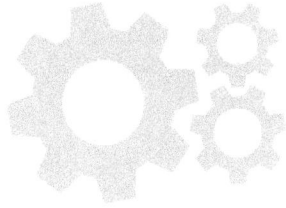

EXPERTS ARE EXEMPLARS

In 1993 professional basketball star Charles Barkley became a spokesperson for Nike. The advertising campaign that followed was controversial.

"I am not a role model," he said, speaking directly into the camera. "I'm not paid to be a role model. I'm paid to wreak havoc on the basketball court. Parents should be role models. Just because I dunk a basketball doesn't mean I should raise your kids."[50]

Despite what Barkley said in the Nike campaign, experts are role models. What an expert does will be copied, mimicked, impersonated, and parroted. Barkley was an exceptional basketball player. Consequently, it would be naive to think that other people, especially young people, would not look to him as a role model.

Most SMEs will not have the same scale of influence as Charles Barkley, but they will have some level of influence throughout their career. Young professionals will watch them for tricks, hints, and nuances. People do what they have seen done, and sometimes experts are watched very closely.

Barkley and Nike may disagree with me, but in my judgment, experts are always exemplars. Always.

65

EXPERTS ARE COUNSELORS

Often SMEs are not the final decision makers. Instead, they are counselors to the decision makers. In these situations, the SME gives guidance and advice, then allows the decision maker to select a course of action.

Helping other people make decisions can be frustrating and discouraging. Helplessly watching as a person rejects or ignores your advice and then suffers needlessly can be agonizing. Unfortunately, it is familiar territory for SMEs. You will be rejected or ignored more than you will be heeded. And, as an SME, the more strongly you cajole decision makers, the more ineffectual your recommendations will become.

As a counselor you cannot force people to do what you want. You can only give them good advice and allow them to govern themselves. Within the limitations of the counseling process, however, there are a few ideas SMEs should follow.

First, lay out the best options. Researchers have shown that experts see more alternatives than other people, they weigh and value each alternative quicker, and they know which alternatives require the least amount of work.[51] Great SMEs consider the many options and then, when they are asked, outline the best options first.

Second, make your recommendation clear. Too often I hear SMEs make two, three, or even ten recommendations for any given problem. Just because you considered the options before making a recommendation doesn't mean your audience must climb your entire decision tree. Cut to the chase. Eliminate unnecessary caveats and qualifiers. Don't hedge. When asked for a recommendation, be bold and unequivocal.

Three, keep your constituents out of trouble. Don't allow your audience to walk blindly off a cliff. One of the responsibilities of SMEs is to protect people and assets from danger. If your recommendation or one of the options a decision maker is considering carries dangers (physical, emotional, mental, financial, political, or otherwise), be sure that person understands it. Be sure the risks are enumerated and appropriately highlighted.

Fourth, avoid the temptation to say, "I told you so." When the decision maker rejects your counsel and eventually tastes the bitter fruit you explicitly warned against, it may be hard not to say those words. But this is when great SMEs stand out. This is when your character and wisdom will be noted. Don't gloat in the disappointment of others.

And fifth, support the decision after it is made. Don't whine and pout about decisions. Even when the decision maker rejects your recommendation, you can almost always find a way to support the decision. A rejected recommendation is not a rejection of you. Nor does it mean that your value to the organization is diminished. To the contrary, decisions are difficult. Leaders rarely keep all their constituents happy. Prove that you can be supportive regardless of which side of the decision you landed on.

Embrace your role as a counselor. Few people get the chance to influence top decision makers, and fewer make a meaningful impact when they do. Lay out the options, offer a clear recommendation, provide appropriate warnings, never use "I told you so," and get behind the decision maker after the decision is made. These ingredients will maximize your impact and increase the likelihood that you will continue to be sought as a counselor.

66

ANECDOTE: BEING A COUNSELOR

I once served as an advisor to a six-hundred-person organization. At one point, the leader, Paul, told me that he needed to select a new manager for his largest department. The person in that position had decided to retire, so Paul was forced to select another person to take the helm. He said to me, "Alan, you know the organization and the people. Who would you recommend as the new department manager?" He added, "Please think about it and give me your recommendation the next time we meet."

As an aside: In situations like this, it is almost always better to give people time to make a thoughtful and thorough recommendation. Rather than forcing me to make a hasty guess with very little forethought, Paul granted me time to consider and weigh the alternatives. His approach conveyed to me that he valued my input and he wanted my best thinking. Good recommendations from SMEs almost always require time to formulate. If decision makers don't grant you sufficient time to prepare your response, ask for the time you need. Sometimes you'll be granted more time and other times not, but it never hurts to ask.

As in many organizations, there were a few obvious internal contenders for the position. Several employees had the skills, intellect, and temperament to do a great job as the department head. Instead of lazily recommending one of the obvious choices, however, I seriously considered every possible alternative. I knew Paul would promote from within his existing organization. So, who should it be? I created and reviewed a list of more than a hundred potential candidates. I reviewed their names and qualifications. Whether the person was twenty years old or seventh, whether they had been in the organization for one year or thirty, I considered the strengths and weaknesses of each, individually. The exercise took considerable time, but the process brought me to one clear recommendation. The conclusion was not what I had expected. I settled on a person who was not on my original list of likely contenders, and who was almost certainly not on Paul's radar.

A week passed and I was scheduled to meet with Paul again. As was always the case, Paul's agenda was full. After discussing other topics, he turned to me and said, "Alan, when we last met, I asked you to prepare a recommendation for this position. Did you do that?"

"Yes, I did."

"Great, what are your thoughts?"

I knew Paul was expecting me to lay out a few options. He expected me to recite the strengths and weaknesses of three or four people. But I had not prepared alternatives; I had prepared a definite recommendation, and I wanted him to seriously consider it without dilution or distraction. So, I paused, squared myself toward Paul, leaned forward in my chair and touched my fingertips together. I looked him straight in the eye and said, "Paul, after careful and lengthy deliberation, I strongly recommend you consider Naomi as the department manager." To emphasize my recommendation, I did not utter another word, nor did I change my posture. I remained fixed in place, fingers together, back straight, chin up, eyes locked. There would be no ambiguity in my message.

After several seconds, Paul broke eye contact and gazed at something else in the room, which gave me permission to relax somewhat. He did not speak for several more seconds. When he did finally speak, he did not reassure me with any follow-up. Instead, he said, "I think that about covers it for today. I'll see you next week." And the meeting was abruptly ended.

We did not speak about the position again until three weeks later when Paul informed me that he was offering Naomi the position. His only feedback was, "You surprised me when you made the recommendation, but the more I thought about it, the more I understood your thinking. Thank you."

When you make a recommendation, make it clear and make it with confidence.

67

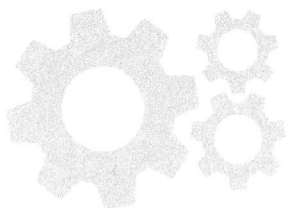

DON'T TALK TOO MUCH

Time is your client's scarcest and most valuable resource. Experts should never waste it, or be surprised or offended when clients try to conserve it. Honoring a client's time is essential to a healthy relationship. Experts who talk too much are disrespectful, and consequently they are avoided. Clients need SMEs to ask concise questions and listen. Then, they need SMEs to selectively and concisely recommend, clarify, and encourage. Great SMEs build trust, establish mutual vision, and ensure delivery, and they do so with a minimum of written and spoken words.

DON'T TALK TOO LITTLE

I t is common for some SMEs to attend meetings, sit quietly for an hour, and depart without saying a word. This practice may protect the expert from assignments, debate, and contention, but it should not be a habit. In rare instances, experts are paid for their silent actions (the courtroom stenographer and the fashion model come to mind), but these are exceptions. Most corporate SMEs are expected to speak.

Of course, talking too little is far better than talking too much, but chronically silent SMEs serve neither their clients nor their colleagues well. When SMEs withhold comment, they diminish their effectiveness and forfeit their influence. It should be the goal of every SME to speak in every meeting.

In fairness, some of our most accomplished experts are severe introverts. They would rather write code or design products than meet with people. Yet, their employers push them into situations that they did not seek and do not enjoy. Just attending a contentious meeting, much less speaking in one, invokes high stress for the naturally silent SME. They would much prefer that others debate ideas, jockey for political position, or wrestle for power. Aggressively pushing for their thoughts to be adopted is simply not what some SMEs relish.

Unfortunately, many organizations and cultures are making matters worse by routinely dismissing the recommendations of the humble SME in favor of the loudmouths or the braggadocios. In these cases, the SMEs might ask themselves, with good reason, "Why bother?"

Furthermore, our hypersensitive, politically charged cultures are pushing SMEs further into silence. Not many years ago when an SME disagreed with someone, it led to a conversation or debate. Today, it can lead to condemnation and social media ridicule.

There is no easy fix for the power struggles that swirl through corporate environments or social media. Domineering hierarchies and social cues can be stifling for all SMEs, particularly for the ones who loathe debate, contention, or ridicule.

Despite the valid justifications for keeping your mouth shut, there are many reasons to speak, and to do it loudly. Here are two such reasons SMEs should speak at every meeting they attend.

First, silence in a meeting implies consent, agreement, or acquiescence. Being silent tells others that you support the accuracy of what has been said, the decisions that others have made, and the consequences of the course being followed. If you do not tell people otherwise, your presence implies agreement.

Second, it takes only a few words to insert your ideas. A few succinct one-word answers or a carefully crafted question can make a huge impact in a crowded meeting. People value the opinion of the SME.

There is a large gap between too much talking by SMEs and too little. Most experts can find the appropriate balance. But if you are an SME who would prefer to remain silent, please remember that your contribution is important, even essential, to the success of your organization. And more important, your attendance and silence imply something even if your words do not. Speak up, not too much, but enough to ensure that your expertise has the right effect.

DON'T CONDESCEND

Regrettably, some experts take pleasure in looking down their noses at their audience. They sit on their high horse and point out the flaws and limitations of the people they should otherwise be helping. Some SMEs think they can be dominant because they gained a little knowledge or skill. But when SMEs interact with an audience, they should do so with sincerity and genuine interest.

No one likes condescension, haughtiness, or contempt. An anonymous internet quote summarizes a typical sentiment toward people like that: "Your pompous attitude and condescending manner have convinced me that you are very smart and terribly important. Said no one, ever."

Condescension is the opposite of humility and is unbecoming of any SME. Yet for some people, condescension is a frequent behavior. Rarely do people intend to be snobs, but they say and do things that come across as arrogant and insensitive. Often, they don't even know they're doing it. Here are ten observations that might help curb your condescending impulses.

OBSERVATION NO. 1: Add to what is said instead of disagreeing with it.

Condescending: "Well, you could do that, but it would actually be a lot better if you did this."

Appropriate: "Yes, you could do that. What other options have you considered?"

Starting with words like *well* and *actually*, implies that you think you are superior.

OBSERVATION NO. 2: Focus rather than minimize.

Condescending: "Simple, all you really need is . . . "

Appropriate: "To ensure I understand, I think you are saying you need this . . . "

Pretending you understand the other party's needs better than they do is always arrogant.

OBSERVATION NO. 3: Listen until you understand.

Condescending: "You did A, B, and C, right?"

Appropriate: "Please explain the sequence you followed."

Allowing other people to speak while you do something else is not listening.

OBSERVATION NO. 4: Don't minimize the contribution of others.

Condescending: "Well, you've got the right idea, but a better approach would be to . . . "

Appropriate: "That's an excellent idea. It is similar to when people do . . . "

Remember that the wisdom of the experts was first taught by someone else.

OBSERVATION NO. 5: Don't insert yourself.

Condescending: "That reminds me of a time when I . . . "

Appropriate: "That's terrific. May I tell other people about your experience?"

It is obvious when SMEs are motivated by glorifying themselves rather than by helping others.

OBSERVATION NO. 6: Don't interrupt.

Condescending: "Well, I think . . . "

Appropriate: Eyes on speaker, mouth shut.

It takes time for people to express their entire thought, so grant them the freedom to do so, at their own pace.

OBSERVATION NO. 7: Be open to alternatives.

Condescending: "Well, I think . . . "

Appropriate: "Please explain that thought further."

Few things are more condescending than an SME who isn't patient enough to listen to the people who make their expertise necessary and valuable.

OBSERVATION NO. 8: Let your audience digest what you've said.

Condescending: "After that you should . . . "

Appropriate: "What questions do you have about that step?"

Don't be so quick to solve a problem that your audience can't remember the first step of the solution.

OBSERVATION NO. 9: Show curiosity.

Condescending: "Yep, I've heard that before . . . "

Appropriate: "Can you tell me more about that?"

Showing interest in a person conveys respect, validation, and humility.

OBSERVATION NO. 10: Say thank you.

Gratitude is a sign of respect. It is hard to be condescending when you are offering genuine appreciation.

No matter how masterful an SME may be, no matter how smart or skilled, there is no long-term benefit to condescension. A smug SME may receive a quick dopamine jolt from humiliating a novice, but the long-term effect is negative for the expert.

At the end of the day, a condescending attitude alienates an SME from friends, superiors, colleagues, and customers. After a decade of snobbery, one highly experienced SME confessed, "I was left feeling smug and superior, but

I was viewed as a petty, snobbish, nit-picking geek by my peers."[52] Don't look down your nose at your audience. Doing so limits your influence and decreases your usefulness. No matter how great you are, or how uninformed your audience may be, don't condescend.

70

EXPERTS DON'T BULLY

Bullies should be rejected at every turn. They are selfish, arrogant, and oppressive. They take out their frustrations on other people and leave hurt, resentment, anger, and depression in their wake. Bullies prey on people they think are weaker than themselves. They seek imbalances of power and use fear, threats, and intimidation to impose their will.

As repugnant as bullying is, almost everyone has had some direct experience with it. It is not isolated to children; adults deal with bullying as well. People experience it online in every digital channel. It happens in the workplace, in politics, the media, and in public discourse.

Experts, it turns out, are just as likely to resort to bullying or manipulation as other people. If that was the end of the story, we would not mention it in this book. But unfortunately, that is not the end of the story. SMEs have important responsibilities in this matter.

By virtue of their unique role, SMEs have power—even significant power—in their organizations. Colleagues are often inclined to comply with an SME's wishes because they believe the SME has unique knowledge and maybe even political clout. But as soon as SMEs push colleagues to comply with their recommendations simply because of their position or authority, rather than by the merits of the recommendation itself, they approach the domain of the bully. People should not do what you say as an SME because you are an expert but because of the merits of what you say. They should be inclined to support you because they know what you recommend helps them, not because your position or power threatens them.

SMEs should never bully colleagues in any way. Being an SME brings special status, but abusing that status destroys trust quickly and will ultimately leave the SME rejected by the people and organizations who should benefit from the SME's service.

71

EXPERTS ARE FRIENDS

The Carnegie Mellon University Center for Entrepreneurial Studies is named after Donald H. Jones, a serial entrepreneur, venture capitalist, and generous contributor to the university. Before his passing in 2012, Jones was a legend on campus and throughout Pittsburgh as a kindhearted mentor to hundreds or thousands of budding entrepreneurs.

One experience I heard Jones share routinely in teaching moments went something like the following: "I was sitting in the lobby at my customer's office waiting for an appointment. As the CEO came out of his office to greet me, he was intercepted by his administrative assistant who handed him a small piece of paper. The CEO stopped, read the paper, wadded it into a ball, tossed it in the wastebasket, and said, 'I don't know who that is. I rarely listen to people I like. Why would I call a person I don't even know?'" The CEO then greeted Jones and led him into his office.

The lesson is that people listen to people they like. Experts can be confident in their facts or data, but if they do not have a relationship, then they work at a disadvantage. The CEO in the anecdote summarized typical behavior honestly: We rarely listen to people we don't like.

Don Jones was a master at making friends. He was disarming, gracious, and kind. Despite his tremendous professional success, he always took an interest in others and made time for them. People listened to Don, in part, because they thought of him as their friend. Great SMEs are friends.

72

MAKE YOUR AUDIENCE FEEL SMART

For several years I have been fortunate to know a history professor at one of our country's great universities. I've seen him field hundreds of questions from large and small audiences. Some of the questions he has been asked have been profound and challenging; others have been downright silly. Yet, in every instance, without exception, he finds a way to acknowledge the questioner and lift that person.

Typically, he elevates a person by using the question as a bridge to a higher-order abstraction or to another important principle. Rather than answering with cold facts, he always elevates.

For example:

Factual answer: "No, I have not actually met George Washington. He died a hundred and fifty years before anyone in this class was born."

Elevating answer: "I have not actually met George Washington, nor has anyone now living, but I think the idea you are getting at is important, and one I have pondered myself. Who are the credible contemporaries of George Washington and what did they say about him?"

SMEs are not diminished when they lift their audience. To the contrary, all parties benefit when the audience is elevated and magnified. SMEs should never hold the mistaken notion that they must seem smarter than the audience to be valuable. When someone asks a question or makes a comment, the SME should respond as positively and respectfully as possible, no matter how dim-witted or ridiculous the question may be.

73

EXPERTS ARE DISPASSIONATE

In his book, *The Death of Expertise: The Campaign against Established Knowledge and Why It Matters*, Tom Nichols writes: "One of the most important characteristics of an expert is the ability to remain dispassionate. Experts must treat everything from cancer to nuclear war as problems to be solved with detachment and objectivity."[53]

Most people, and especially SMEs, prefer sobriety and objectivity when dealing with critical issues. Emotions often lead to irrational arguments, erroneous conclusions, and bad decisions. Consequently, many of the world's greatest thinkers recommend, like Nichols, that experts should exercise restraint.

Dr. Marcia Angell, former editor-in-chief of the *New England Journal of Medicine*, for example, wrote that the appointment of a dispassionate panel of experts to evaluate the strength of scientific evidence is a model that should be emulated.[54] Other critics have said something similar.[55] [56]

Ironically, Nichols is hardly dispassionate himself. On the contrary, he is a highly passionate person who is not shy about sharing his opinions. Of his book, the *Financial Times* wrote, "His anger is a lot more attractive than the standard condescension." It is no surprise that the first testimonial printed inside the book starts with the word "impassioned."

As an author on the subject of expertise, Nichols made an impassioned plea for experts to be dispassionate. I love that. This paradox is not unique to Nichols or his book. All SMEs must face the dilemma of emotional response. On one hand, we expect our experts to be poker-faced and objective. On the other hand, passion is often more persuasive than logic.

While Nichols espouses dispassion in the face of cancer or even nuclear war, I for one believe that cancer and nuclear war warrant a little passion. Many of the same people who want experts to be solid as bedrock also want them to be ardent and spirited. We need our experts to show fire in the belly and a twinkle in the eye. Sometimes SMEs are most effective with a voice of thunder that shakes the earth. Winston Churchill was not trying to show his dispassionate side when he said, "Never give in, never, never, never—never, in nothing, great or small, large or petty—never give in except to convictions of honor and good sense."[57]

Experts need to be dispassionate yet passionate, gentle yet forceful, humble yet brimming with confidence. Tom Nichols offered sound advice when he said that experts should have *the ability* to remain dispassionate, but he also showed through example that they must also have the wisdom to go beyond unemotional detachment when appropriate.

74

EXPERTS HONOR CONFIDENTIALITY

Great SMEs don't disclose their company's secret information, nor do they disclose the secrets of their customers or partners to unauthorized parties—period. Nothing else on this subject should need to be said.

Keeping confidences is not always that simple, however. If it were, our news feeds would not be brimming daily with unauthorized disclosures from government agencies and company executives. WikiLeaks and Julian Assange would never have risen to global notoriety.

Why do all large organizations grapple with violations of confidence? Keeping secrets, it turns out, is difficult to do. Sigmund Freud wrote in 1905, "No mortal can keep a secret. If his lips are silent, he chatters with his finger-tips; betrayal oozes out of him at every pore."[58]

For many psychological and emotional reasons, it is more difficult to keep a secret than it is to disclose it. People have a natural propensity to tell. We are hardwired to share what we know, and filtering information that should not be disclosed can be tedious and burdensome. Researchers have determined that the bigger the secret, the harder it is to keep.[59]

Often in my career I have been in meetings where customers seek confidential information from SMEs. They ask something along the lines of "We know you're providing service to our competition. What are they planning to do with this technology?" With this simple inducement, many SMEs will then spill the beans.

Some SMEs acknowledge that they are violating a confidence, but they do it anyway. I've heard SMEs say things like, "Well, I am not authorized to tell you who is doing this, but there might be a major social media company whose name rhymes with Gracebook who is doing this." As if the SME is not violating a confidence by using thinly veiled language! This approach is hardly confidential.

If Freud was correct in 1905 that mortals could not keep secrets, the problem is undoubtedly worse today. Our digital world is overflowing with mechanisms tuned for disclosure. Our devices allow us to communicate with our lips and chatter with our fingertips. At times, smartphones do indeed ooze with betrayal.

SMEs needn't be examples of Freudian psychology. They can, they should, they must keep confidences.

75

WHEN YOU CAN TELL

In the last chapter I asserted that SMEs should honor confidentiality. There are, of course, exceptions. Not all confidential information needs to remain undisclosed. The circumstances that justify disclosure, however, are rare and easily identified. Here are the three circumstances when SMEs can openly tell others what was obtained in confidence.

First, if confidential information is later disclosed publicly through no wrongful act, it is no longer confidential. This should be obvious but is frequently overlooked. Frequently, SMEs obtain information in confidence and they assume it will be confidential forever. It rarely is. Even top-secret military records are eventually declassified. SMEs should remain attuned to the public information in their industry, especially about their clients. Information that was previously protected often becomes publicly available.

Second, the law may require at least limited disclosure of private information. Mandatory reporting laws in instances of abuse require some SMEs to report illegal behavior. In my experience, legally required disclosures are rare and should only be performed after obtaining appropriate legal counsel.

Third, SMEs can obtain permission to disclose confidential information directly from the other party. Just because your clients don't want to disclose information themselves does not automatically mean that they don't want you to disclose the information either. This is particularly true with client successes.

A company may not be inclined to boast of its own accomplishments, but it may be comfortable allowing others to speak for it. A wise advisor once told me, "Every time you receive confidential information that makes someone look good, seek permission to share the experience." I have been surprised at how frequently people say yes.

Even when one of these three exceptions apply, SMEs still should not disclose confidential information without documented evidence of the exception. Verbal authorization is rarely enough. In the absence of documented justification, SMEs should never disclose confidential information. Ever.

76

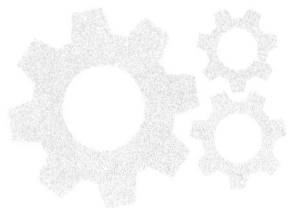

KEEP THINGS SECURE

When an expert touches something, whether physically, digitally, or in some other way, it bears their fingerprints. Thereafter, any lapse in security or any disclosure can and often will be traced to the SME's protective care. That's why SMEs should never be careless with valuable assets.

SMEs don't leave doors open when they should be locked, so they shouldn't leave documents on their desk if they should be stored in a drawer and they shouldn't cut corners when securing their computers. SMEs must keep valuable assets secure.

I once worked with a senior software architect who was also a highly trained computer security expert. He was in demand by clients and colleagues to fix their most vexing information security issues. Because of his expertise, he was granted carte blanche access to his employer's networks.

One day a compromise was detected inside the company. After careful review, an innocuous server was found under the security expert's desk. The server, it turns out, had been hacked by foreign actors and was being used to launch attacks on the rest of the company's network. The team that monitored the company network knew about the server but assumed the expert had a purpose in keeping it on the network. Like a plumber who does not maintain the pipes in his own house, the expert neglected the server as it aged, and it became vulnerable. Had the server been in anyone else's care, the company's security team would have most certainly shut it down, but because they trusted the expert, they allowed the sloppy maintenance to persist. Remarkably, the expert kept his job, but trust was compromised.

Few things will destroy trust faster than carelessness. SMEs should never be careless, especially with valuable assets.

77

AVOID TECHNICAL JARGON

G reat SMEs master the vocabulary of their trade. It's vital that they know the grammar and syntax of their domain and that they can articulate ideas with the correct language. Vocabulary is a key indicator of expertise. People judge you by the words you use. One of the quickest ways to destroy your credibility as an expert is by not using proper industry jargon.

Many years ago, I was with a colleague at a large industry event. We were listening to a technology reporter talk about a new computer system. When the reporter referenced the hard drives in the system, he said it contained "S-C-S-I drives." I chuckled to myself because even though the acronym is spelled SCSI, it was commonly pronounced "skuh-zee." My colleague, on the other hand, was aghast. He looked at me and said, "This guy has no idea what he's talking about." He then walked way, dismissing the journalist and everything he said. The journalist lost all credibility by not knowing one acronym.

So, if you're going to use jargon, make sure you use it correctly, especially in front of a knowledgeable audience. Of course, just because you know jargon doesn't mean you should always use it. Many SMEs tend to overuse technical language. They have the misconception that the more jargon a person uses, the more knowledgeable they appear. The more obscure the acronyms, the better. The truly valuable expert knows that accurate understanding is far more important than technical mumbo jumbo. If your audience knows the jargon, then fine, use it. But with larger audiences or with audiences comprising people with varied skill levels, there is almost always someone who doesn't know what you are talking about.

Using jargon will not buttress your genius or fully conceal a deficiency in knowledge, either. Far too often, aspiring experts hide their limited knowledge beneath layers of complicated, abstract, or voluminous language.

Acronym-laden comments often confound rather than enlighten an audience. Great experts don't spew jargon. They don't yammer about complex items hoping the audience will acquiesce. Great experts employ words that people will understand.

78

AVOID SAYING NO

In April 2018 Mark Zuckerberg, the founder and CEO of Facebook, appeared before members of the United States Senate to answer questions about his company. During the two-day hearing, forty-nine elected officials asked Zuckerberg hundreds of detailed questions. Most of the questions were polar, meaning they could have been answered with a yes or a no. But Zuckerberg rarely answered that way. He almost always avoided definite binary responses, even in those instances when lawmakers insisted on a yes or a no.[60]

Take for example the exchange between Zuckerberg and Senator Ed Markey about new laws protecting children:

Markey: "Would you support a privacy bill of rights for kids where opt-in is the standard? Yes or no?"

Zuckerberg: "Senator, I think that that's an important principle and . . . "

Markey: "I appreciate that."

Zuckerberg: "And I think we should."

Markey: "But we need a law to protect those children. That's my question to you. Do you think we need a law to do so? Yes or no?"

Zuckerberg: "Senator, I'm not sure if we need a law, but I think that this is certainly a thing that deserves a lot of discussion."

When a questioner insists on a yes or no answer, as Markey did, the question is almost always a trap. The truth is far more complicated. Facebook's support for a law protecting children would almost certainly depend on the merits of the law. If Zuckerberg said yes, people would expect Facebook to support any law regardless of its provisions. If Zuckerberg said no, people would accuse him of not caring for children. This was a trick question. Zuckerberg recognized it as such and responded appropriately.

Later in the same hearing, Senator Gary Peters also insisted on a yes or no answer. This time Zuckerberg stepped in the trap and had to retreat immediately.

Peters: "Yes or no, does Facebook use audio obtained from mobile devices to enrich personal information about its users?"

Zuckerberg: "No. [pause] Well, [pause] Senator, [pause] let me be—let me be clear on this."

As Zuckerberg illustrates, it is rare that answering a question with a definitive no is an SME's best option. If it's possible to answer honestly without saying no, then do so. The word *no* doesn't just feel negative; it connotes rejection, failure, and contention. It often pits two sides against each other and precludes possible alternatives. No is final and definitive. No is almost always the end.

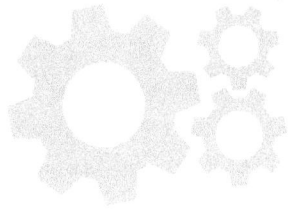

79

FIND YES

I was once in a meeting with the CEO and the chief technology officer of a medium-sized company. Also on the call were members of their technology and marketing teams. The CEO, named Gary, and the marketing team wanted to change the company's pricing models, but they anticipated the company's financial systems would not support their plans. The conversation between Gary and the CTO, Anderson, went something like this:

"We need to introduce new pricing as soon as possible. Can the financial systems support bundled pricing?" Gary asked.

"No," Anderson responded, "they cannot."

"Of course not. How silly of me!" Gary responded sarcastically. "Can they support subscription-based pricing?"

"No, they cannot," Anderson replied again.

There was a protracted pause. Eventually Gary spoke again, "Anderson, I hate it when you do this. *Stop* being so stubbornly literal! Stop forcing me to ask questions in exactly the right way before we get to the answer we need."

Anderson seemed shocked and responded, "Gary, I'm not forcing you to do anything. I'm simply answering your questions."

"Is that right?" Gary sniped.

"Yes, it is."

"Okay, how about this question?" Gary continued. "If we postpone another strategic project and free up engineering resources, can your team modify the financial systems to support bundled and subscription pricing?"

Anderson paused only briefly before responding, "Yes, we can."

"Yes?!" Gary quipped. "Wow, finally! Fantastic. Why couldn't you say that in the first place?"

"That's not what you asked."

Laypeople, including some corporate leaders, at times complain that SMEs torture them with precise language. It is common for an SME's blunt no answer to be interpreted as stonewalling, or worse yet, adversarial or hostile.

Of course, SMEs have the right to use candid language unapologetically. A byproduct of expertise is precision; therefore, it is natural for SMEs to prefer exactness, including a generous allotment of noes. But SMEs should not be surprised when laypeople, including executives, respond negatively to their exactitude.

SMEs often learn late in their careers that you can accomplish the same results with a yes as you can with a no, and your audience will be much happier during and after the conversation. Take the example I just shared. Rather than saying no to virtually everything Gary asked, I believe that Anderson could have achieved the same result while using a more agreeable tone.

Gary: "Can the financial systems support bundled pricing?"

Anderson: "As we all know, the current financial systems are constraining and brittle. They do not support bundled pricing, nor do they support subscriptions. But, yes, we might be able to adjust. How important is this pricing strategy?"

Gary: "It's important, obviously, or we wouldn't be talking about it."

Anderson: "I see. Yes, we can assign engineers to change the financial systems, but that will take them away from other strategic initiatives. Are the pricing changes more important than our team's current assignments?"

Gary: "Yes, pricing is the top priority."

Anderson: "OK. Yes, if we delay the other projects, we can modify the financial systems to support the pricing the company needs."

I have been impressed at how effective yes can be and amazed at how much more productive a dialogue can be when SMEs apply this simple concept. Look for ways to say yes.

80

EXCEPTIONS TO YES

There are, of course, a few exceptions to looking for yes. As outlined in the last chapter, SMEs should look for ways to say yes when they interact with a friendly audience, such as customers or colleagues. They shouldn't look for yes, on the other hand, when communicating with adversaries. Rarely do competitors or detractors merit cooperation. Courtesy certainly, but helpfulness? Sorry, not so much. They don't deserve a definitive yes or no. SMEs should look for yes when the audience warrants it.

Legal conversations require special caution. Courtrooms and depositions are not the place for SMEs to portion out generous servings of yesses. Conversations with judges, law enforcement officers, and lawyers necessitate honesty and candor but not reckless cooperation. Miranda rights in the United States should stand as a warning to all SMEs when dealing with the law: "Anything you say can and will be used against you." Don't say yes to those who seek your destruction.

DON'T CRITICIZE COLLEAGUES

SMEs do not criticize their colleagues or dismiss what they say, especially not in front of customers. SMEs should be agents of unity, not division. They should constantly seek opportunities to agree. When you do agree, acknowledge it, point it out, emphasize it, and celebrate it.

We live in a time of hypercriticism. Politicians, pundits, and professionals of many disciplines have demonstrated that contests can be won through cutting criticism. Don't buy into it. Finding fault with your colleagues doesn't help you and it doesn't help them. Even when you're right, criticism hurts them and soils you. Don't do it.

WIIO'S LAW

E dward Murphy is the aerospace engineer from the 1940s and 1950s who is credited with the adage, "Anything that can go wrong will go wrong." Now referred to as "Murphy's Law," the message captures a truth that is as old as human history. Every SME should know and respect the universal application of Murphy's Law.

To emphasize that Murphy's Law applies to failings in communication as much as it does to any other discipline, Osmo Wiio, a Finnish academic and author, amended Murphy's Law with a sarcastic set of communication axioms called Wiio's laws. He stated, "Communication usually fails, except by accident." And, more important, "If a message can be interpreted in several ways, it will be interpreted in a manner that maximizes the damage."[61]

Many SMEs acknowledge Murphy but ignore Wiio. They know that physical products fail, software contains bugs, and people make mistakes. Because of these shortcomings, they plan accordingly. But the same SMEs assume their own utterances are clear and their email is always convincing. Few SMEs consider their own communication failings. Great SMEs constantly ask themselves if their explanations are understood and how they can correct misunderstandings. They expect their communications to fail and patiently prepare for repetition, clarification, examples, and illustrations. They recognize that people rarely understand new concepts on the first explanation, so they prepare multiple ones.

If anything can go wrong, it will go wrong, and that includes everything you say and everything you write. Plan on it.

83

TEST EVERYTHING

Never trust opinions, not even your own. Be suspicious of data, especially your own. Question the consensus. Fear everything and test always. Maintain intellectual honesty and always examine both sides of the hypothesis.

Wernher von Braun was a NASA aerospace engineer and rocket pioneer who is credited with saying: "One good test is worth a thousand expert opinions." Perform the test and consider the results. Adjust the test and perform the test again. Believe the results of a test before you believe an opinion. Embrace and promote the results of tests.

DON'T THROW PEOPLE
UNDER THE BUS

Nearly everyone has experienced or at least witnessed it. You make a mistake, and a person who should have been an ally broadcasts your error to a large audience or, worse, to a senior member of your team, with the intent of convicting you and acquitting themselves. Nobody likes this form of betrayal, but the practice is epidemic. Regardless of its frequency or justification, throwing people under the bus is unbecoming of an SME. It is a violation of trust, and SMEs should never violate trust.

As an observer of experts, I find this subject particularly entertaining. It turns out that throwing an SME under the bus is masochistic. It's comparable to a high school basketball player challenging LeBron James to a one-on-one contest. Or like watching someone get in the face of Ultimate Fighting Championship star Conor McGregor. Or like hearing someone mutter that Olympic champion sprinter Usain Bolt is slow. Fools make these assertions, and often it is the fool who tries to throw the SME under the bus. But fools don't merit retaliation. James proves nothing by dunking over a high school player. McGregor proves nothing by knocking out some obnoxious drunk. Bolt shouldn't lace his shoes for the vast majority of us. Regardless of how tempting it may be to shred a foolish challenger, don't do it.

An SME is an advocate, a supporter, and an ally. They gain trust because they always lift and support; they never destroy or tear down. They can be trusted, not just when it is easy, but also when it is hard. When stress gets high, when other people are looking for political cover, the SME is a steadfast supporter and friend. Even when the SME is betrayed and left to swing in the breeze, even when the SME knows where all the blame actually lies, or even when the SME could easily dodge the bullet and cast someone else to the dogs, they never throw anyone under the bus.

85

PRAISE

The praise of an expert carries weight and meaning. When an expert genuinely expresses approval, admiration, or commendation, it is felt by the recipient, sometimes with profound personal effect.

I remember when a professor whom I respected complimented me for a lecture I delivered. His handwritten note was simple and kind, but genuine. Because I held him in high regard, his applause was particularly impactful to me. Years later, I still find reassurance in his note.

SMEs do not just avoid blame, as we covered in the last chapter. They look for ways to compliment and lift people. We are surrounded by people who are starved for recognition or appreciation. Too few managers and leaders reward their teammates with the praise they want or deserve. A thoughtful gesture, especially from an esteemed SME, can produce profound inspiration and motivation.

Be an SME who is generous with praise. It costs you very little but gives the recipient untold benefit.

86

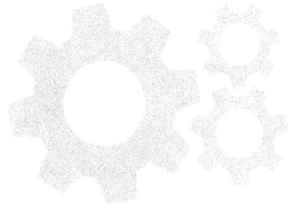

DON'T SCARE PEOPLE

I once met with a man who was appointed by the Obama administration to oversee the operation of all US military spy satellites. Every morning he received a top-secret report about hostile activities throughout the world. During the meeting I asked him, "What do you wish people knew about our world?" He paused for a long time, and with sustained eye contact, he lifted his hand and touched his fingers to his thumb. "I wish," he said, then paused again. "I wish people knew just how dangerous this world is and how much risk there is to freedom-loving people everywhere."

Fear is a powerful motivator. It influences our decisions and our behavior. It affects the actions of children on a schoolyard playground as well as the entire military industrial complex. Fear is prevalent in political debate for both candidates and causes. It is used to pressure people into buying medication, insurance, security systems, and even new tires and toothpaste. Because of its profound influence, sales and marketing organizations routinely contemplate the influence of fear in their clients' buying process. Marketers know that customers who are afraid pay closer attention, are more likely to buy, and will do so more quickly than customers who are not. No human emotion impacts buying behavior more dramatically than fear.

SMEs often have a front row seat to the fear show. Experts know the specifics of what people should fear and what they should not. They know when uncertainty is high and, conversely, when risk is contained. Furthermore, experts have the luxury of observing circumstances from a position of experience, objectivity, and distance, and consequently, they can use their authority to energetically stoke fear or calmly subdue it. Experts can be the bearers of trouble and anxiety or the bearers of reassurance and peace.

There are certainly times when an expert must frighten an audience. Candor and honesty demand it. The oncologist sows fear when informing a patient that cancer is present. The network operator sows fear when informing management that a server was hacked. The weather reporter sows fear when predicting the path of a hurricane.

While it is true that experts may need to deliver dire, solemn, and frightening news, it is my observation that great experts help their audience move beyond fear. Great SMEs don't deliver bad news and walk away. To the contrary, they know that fear is an emotional response to uncertainty and can be overcome through logic, reason, reassurance, encouragement, and patience. Great experts recognize fear when it appears and move quickly to vanquish it. The late political columnist Charles Krauthammer once wrote, "The omniscient have no fear."[62]

The fearful expert may inspire critical thinking and knee-jerk sales in the short run, but relationships built on fear eventually end badly. Fear-mongering experts will be rejected and despised. Experts who only identify and accentuate problems will be, and always are, replaced by experts who identify and accentuate the solutions to those problems.

DETERMINE MUTUAL VISION

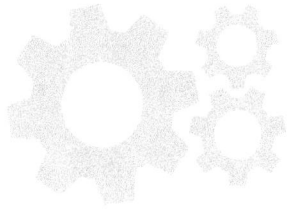

87

VISION

Experts can see things that other people cannot.

We established in the previous section that a top priority for a subject matter expert is to establish trust. Immediately thereafter it is to define a common vision. Seeing what your customer needs and then helping them obtain that desired future is the mark of a truly exceptional and valuable SME.

Many years ago, I worked as a programmer at a large software development company. I worked with some exceptionally talented technical people. One day I entered a colleague's office and found three programmers huddled around a computer monitor.

On the screen was the hex dump of a program they were working on. (For those not familiar, a hex dump is a hexadecimal representation of computer memory. Here is a hex dump of my name, Alan Berrey: 416c616e20426572726579)

The senior programmer was pointing at the screen filled with the hex dump and translating the code into English in his mind, saying, "Move A2 to A1. Compare A1 to A3. Jump to . . . " Then he stopped suddenly. "Wait! There it is!" He pointed at a code on a screen that looked like 84C2. "That pointer is wrong!"

I quickly realized that this senior programmer could see something that I could not. He could view hexadecimal code, translate it into English, and traverse the program in his mind. This is a unique and, in the right circumstances, useful skill.

Vision, it turns out, is a universal attribute of expertise. Experts see things that other people do not see. This is not to say that experts have superior visual acuity. They see the same things as everyone else, but they have superior perception of what they see.

Take for example the radiologist at a hospital. This person is trained to recognize features in images that are not obvious to the rest of us. The radiologist sees things that we do not see. Not because the image that the radiologist is looking at is any different than the one we are looking at, but because the radiologist is able to apply refined judgment.

It is proven that expert tennis players see a serve differently from the average tennis hobbyist.[63] Chess masters see a game arrangement differently than average players.[64] Expert painters see art differently than average observers.[65]

So, SMEs should routinely ask themselves, "Given what I see, what do I perceive or know about this situation? And, given that perception, how will people be better as a consequence of working with me? How will their future improve?

Expert vision is what your audience needs from you and your expert vision should include three things:

1. A potential future state, or a clear idea of what is and is not possible.

2. A correct representation of the characteristics and attributes of that future state. Not some Pollyanna representation, but a clear, concrete model.

3. A path to accomplishing that state, as desired.

In this section we'll cover many of the ideas that SMEs will use to capitalize on their unique vision and convey their vision to customers and colleagues in compelling ways.

88

ANECDOTE: VISION

Years ago, I attended a meeting with a prospective client and an SME who worked as a network and information security operations manager. The SME was brought into the meeting to help convince the customer that they should entrust their company data center services to the SME's company. The SME was highly qualified and intelligent. He came across as confident and professional. It was obvious to me that the client believed the SME could accomplish what the company thought they needed. Toward the end of the meeting, however, a client representative said, "I think your team may be overqualified. You can obviously do far more than we need at the moment."

In response, the SME changed the customer's vision. He said something like the following: "I can see how you might think that, but I hope you'll allow me to challenge that thinking for a moment. You need the skills of the people in this room, and then some. It is not the problem you are facing today that you or I should worry about. It is the problem you will be facing tomorrow. It is that problem, tomorrow's problem, the problem that is bigger and more urgent than today's problem. It is that problem that should be addressed today, and we are the team who can address it. If you only want to worry about today's problems, then you might be right. We might not be the team for you. But if you want to get in front of tomorrow's problems then I believe we can help you, and we can do it today."

89

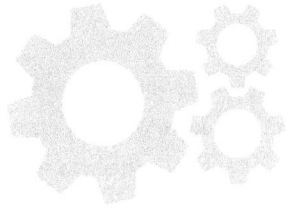

EXPECTATIONS

Our lives are filled with expectations. From our earliest age, our actions are shaped and modified by the explicit and implicit expectations of the people and institutions around us. Our parents and friends expect certain behavior, and our employers do as well. Our governments impose expectations through laws. From the moment of our birth, a mountain of expectations falls upon us, and the burdens associated with those expectations only grows.

Expectations, of course, are ignored or forgotten after they are realized. I expect the light to come on when I flip the switch. I expect the car to start when I turn the key. I expect the grocer to carry my favorite yogurt. But when expectations are not realized, we are faced with a conundrum. Why is my expectation misaligned with reality? What did I get wrong? Why have other people let me down? How can this circumstance be rectified?

It would be logical if our emotional reaction to missed expectations was proportionate to the real cost, but often our emotions are exaggerated. For example, when I open the kitchen drawer and I do not find a utensil in its appointed location, the actual harm I experience is quite small, but for some people that triggers a response of unwarranted negativity.

When the circumstances are larger than a misplaced utensil, we can experience an explosion of negative emotional energy. We can become frustrated, depressed, angry, anxious, frightened, or shocked. This is all because the way we perceive the world is wrong in some way. Imagine, for example, that you are driving to work anticipating several important client meetings. At an intersection someone runs a red light and strikes your vehicle. Fortunately, no one is injured but your automobile is seriously damaged and unable to function. You immediately realize your expectations for the day will not be realized. The more you consider your current plight, the more you realize just how far-reaching the consequences of the accident are. The car will need to be repaired or replaced. The meetings, events, and appointments that were accessible before the accident are instantly out of reach without the assistance of others. Your schedule will be affected today, tomorrow, and potentially many more days that follow. The accident will be inconvenient and potentially expensive to remedy. How would you react under the circumstances?

Expectations shape our behavior and inform our emotional response to events in our lives. When our expectations are not realized, it can be highly distressing, often disproportionately so.

Herein is an important lesson for SMEs. Audiences come with expectations for an SME—they hope the SME will rectify a certain problem. If there were no expectations, there would be no need for an SME. Your goal as an SME, therefore, is to satisfy your audience's expectations. It is not enough to perform the task that you think is needed. You must perform the task your audience thinks will satisfy their perceived needs.

Of course, it is not always possible for SMEs to fully satisfy an audience's expectations. A medical patient may expect a doctor to eliminate all the pain associated with an ailment, for example. This may not be possible or desirable. Nevertheless, an SME starts with the objective of satisfying the audience's hopes and expectations. If you can't or don't meet their expectations, then you should be prepared for an explosion of negative emotional energy.

90

EXPERTS ARE PROPHETS

Expertise is by definition prophetic. It is knowing, "This is where we are, and that is where we will go."

References to prophecy may conjure religious imagery. Indeed, the most famous prophets in history are religious figures, including Jesus Christ, the Apostle Paul, Abraham, Muhammad, Moses, and Noah. But prophecy is not only a religious phenomenon. Oracles and prophets are a recurring theme in legends, fairy tales, books, and movies throughout the world. Whether it is Neo seeking to see the future through the Oracle in *The Matrix*, or Dorothy seeking to control the future by following the yellow brick road to the Wizard of Oz, the prophet predicts and controls the future. Legends teach that only fools ignore the decrees of the prophets.

The phenomenon of prophecy extends to secularists. They also predict the future, as they must. Nutritionists prophesy health, mechanical engineers prophesy safety, and climate scientists prophesy temperature, to list just a few. They are all purveyors of predictions, often personalized once. Besides telling the future for the masses, they prophesy the future for individuals.

In the role of prophet, the SME has a daunting responsibility. Most of us can't predict our own future, much less the future of others. But that is exactly what the world expects of the expert: specific, accurate, reliable, repeatable prophecy. If SMEs cannot see and influence the future, then they are of little use to the people they serve. When a doctor prescribes a medication, or a general contractor recommends a type of construction, or a CEO hires a team of professionals, they are all predicting the future. They may not fully control that future, but they are taking actions with the specific intention of obtaining a desired condition in the future. Yes, SMEs must be prophets.

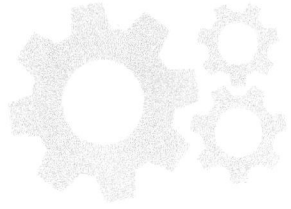

91

AS I STATED PREVIOUSLY

Experts know that people learn through repetition. The chances are high that your audience will not understand everything you say the first time. Plan on restating your key messages. Remember that people learn at different speeds. Be patient throughout the process.

92

EXPERTS SIMPLIFY

Experts are notorious for making things more complicated than necessary. If there is one stereotype about experts that they should avoid, it is that they magnify complexity, or use the most complex form possible to explain something or answer a question. Experts constantly fall into the trap of complicating things. When asked a question that just requires a short, direct answer, for example, experts often launch into a lengthy diatribe that they believe demonstrates their superior knowledge. Unfortunately, complexity often hurts more than it helps.

The problems presented to experts are often very complicated, but the wisest experts see problems in their simplest form, explain those problems in the simplest language, and solve them with the simplest solutions. Simplify, simplify, simplify!

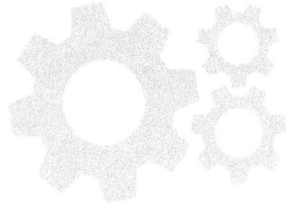

STAY OUT OF THE WEEDS

Years ago, while working at a large information technology consulting company, I attended a meeting with one of our customers, Blue Cross Blue Shield. Also in attendance was a senior engineer from my company named Bret. During the meeting someone asked Bret a question about the billing system. I could feel a collective groan sweep over my colleagues. Bret immediately launched into the tortuous details of database deadlocks, the proper use of semaphores, and the pros and cons of non-relational databases in high-volume accounting systems.

In the correct setting, Bret's comments would have been perfectly appropriate and interesting. There was, technically speaking, nothing wrong with his comments. With our clients, however, Bret was completely bogged down in the details. One by one the client team's faces glazed over. Our sales director put his face in his hands and moaned in dismay.

Bret knew his comments were not valued. He said to me later, "Alan, I know people want me to stay out of the weeds, but it is difficult when they don't know anything, and the answer is complicated."

It can be difficult for smart people who understand complicated subjects to keep their explanations simple. Performing that task well, however, is precisely what distinguishes great SMEs from mediocre ones.

Great SMEs always tailor their comments to the skills of their audience and the context of the situation. They rarely go into the weeds.

EXPERTS ARE
MASTER TEACHERS

The best experts are great teachers. They love the subject of their expertise and enjoy sharing their knowledge and skills with others. They gain satisfaction in the improved performance of their colleagues, friends, and students, and find it gratifying to teach and to be emulated.

Great SMEs have a genuine desire to help others avoid the hard knocks they themselves experienced while attaining their expertise. They help others accelerate their learning and avoid predictable pitfalls, roadblocks, and needless pain. They encourage others to exceed their own accomplishments and support them to that end.

There is one attribute of master teachers that all experts should emulate: They teach principles and truths that endure. They don't just teach the facts, the dos and don'ts, or the how-tos of something. No, master teachers have the unique capacity to teach concepts and ideas that have lasting value. Every domain of knowledge can be taught on the foundation of timeless principles, and master teachers can distill and deliver these principles. This attribute unfailingly distinguishes a merely good teacher from the undisputed expert.

Cheap teaching is like cheap food: It fills the stomach but offers little enduring nutritional value. The master teacher knows what knowledge is cheap and what knowledge is valuable. The master teacher knows what knowledge offers short-term benefits or gratification and what brings enduring guidance. Remember, for the great SME, what matters most is what matters longest.

METAPHORS AND ANALOGIES

Experts can find it difficult to explain their ideas to non-experts. Even when people work in the same industry and use similar vocabulary, communication is chancy. One approach for explaining complex ideas is to use effective metaphors and analogies. Creative metaphors can be far more helpful and convincing than exhaustively detailed explanations. Take, for example, terms like *the web*, *cloud computing*, and *data mining*. They convey technical concepts using words that people can at least partially understand and explore.

Years ago, I listened to an SME talk about the importance of information security at his company. He was trying to make the point that despite common perception, proper data security is not designed to slow everything down inside a company. He argued that effective security should help accelerate the business. Unfortunately, his colleagues weren't buying it. They quickly enumerated several information security policies that, in their judgment, slowed them down and made it more difficult to perform their jobs. One colleague said, "I got locked out of the network last week and it took hours for my account to be restored."

Fortunately, the SME had a masterful analogy prepared. "Information security is like the brakes in your car," he explained. "Yes, brakes slow you down, but without them, you could not drive the way you do. It is the combination of brakes and the engine that enable fast transportation; neither is effective without the other." With one carefully placed analogy, the argument was over.

As an SME, you might find it helpful to have a repertoire of pithy analogies and metaphors. Rather than using verbose commentary about complicated subjects, allow these abstractions to make your points for you. Try them out and discard the ones that don't work effectively. Adjust the ones that do. Write them down.

A metaphor or an analogy, you see, is like computer memory; it stores massive amounts of information in a tiny package.

DON'T SURPRISE

Don't surprise your clients or your colleagues.

Surprises might be okay from SMEs if they bring good news such as, "Surprise! We just discovered a cure for our largest vexing problem!" Or, "Surprise! We just discovered life on another planet." But typically, surprises are bad.

Great experts always give people a warning before delivering bad news. They don't drop bad news out of the sky, especially not in a group setting. Things will go much better if your audience has time to prepare.

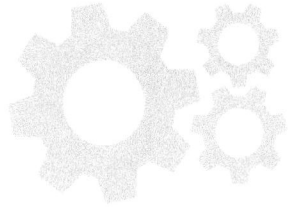

97

BE TEMPERATE

The finest glass is tempered. The glass is run through an oven and heated to 620 degrees Celsius (1,148 degrees Fahrenheit). It then undergoes a high-pressure cooling procedure that lasts just a few seconds. High-pressure air is blasted onto the glass cooling the outer surface much more quickly than the center. As the center of the glass cools, it pulls back from the outer surface, resulting in fixed tension. This permanent pressure gives tempered glass its strength.

Standard annealed glass breaks at about six thousand pounds per square inch. Tempered glass, on the other hand, generally breaks at approximately twenty-four thousand pounds per square inch.

Temperance is an often-overlooked personal attribute that experts should develop. Being temperate means you are self-restrained and not given to extreme opinions. Being temperate means you are measured in your positions, balanced in your opinion, and controlled in your reactions. Regardless of the conflict or the intensity of the situation, you remain calm, poised, and dignified. Tempered experts don't fly off the handle, they don't shatter, and they don't break. They are resilient, transparent, and tough. Great experts are temperate.

98

ASSUME IGNORANCE
BEFORE MALICE

They did it because they are stupid, not because they are wicked.

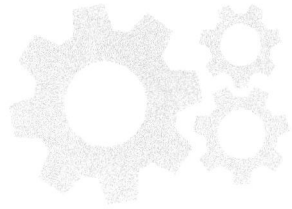

99

DON'T IGNORE

Everyone in the room is important. Acknowledge every comment and validate every question. If someone is being ignored then focus your attention, if only temporarily, on that person. Ensure that everyone feels heard.

A professor of history once explained to me that the most effective forms of teaching all begin with listening. You have a much better chance of changing someone's mind if you allow them to speak until they feel heard, rather than if you speak until they are exhausted.

ENSURE DELIVERY

100

DELIVER THE GOODS

SMEs must deliver value to their customers, colleagues, and partners. They must constantly and convincingly provide a service that other people cannot easily replicate. Nothing is more important. When an SME says a new technology will be launched, it is. When an SME predicts that cost and quality metrics will be realized, they are. And, when an SME says it will rain, it rains. One of the surest ways to lose credibility is by failing to deliver on expectations. Whether a commitment is small or large, simple or complicated, SMEs must find a way to deliver the goods and do so repeatedly.

Even though perfection is unattainable, great SMEs pursue it. Kobe Bryant did not make every game-winning shot he attempted in the NBA. And Abby Wambach did not score with every header she attempted in soccer. But during their remarkable careers, Bryant and Wambach were sought as experts because they delivered points in big ways and in clutch situations. When the game was on the line and the stakes were high, fans, players, and coaches all knew their best chance of winning was by putting the ball under the control of their experts. If anyone could deliver points, Bryant and Wambach could.

This fits a theory in team sports that the ball is given to the experts who others believe will deliver points. You only need to watch a pickup game of basketball or soccer at a city park to see this dynamic in action. When newcomers join a team, they are granted a short test period to prove themselves. If a new player immediately performs well, they are given the ball again. If they miss their shots or turn the ball over, their teammates will then stop passing the ball to them and their opportunities will dry up.

This dynamic is true for almost all SMEs in all industries. If you deliver points for your team, then you will be given additional opportunities to score. Your reward for delivering on a commitment is the opportunity to make and keep additional commitments. The more an SME delivers for their company, the more they will be given opportunities to deliver again. If they fail to deliver, the opportunities will disappear, and the next opportunity will be passed to another SME.

When things go wrong, SMEs don't make excuses. They don't point fingers at colleagues who miss deadlines or suppliers who failed to ship products. No one cares if the grass was wet when Wambach tried to score in soccer or if an opponent's hand was in Bryant's face when he attempted a game-winning three-pointer. Great SMEs don't point to reasons for missed delivery. They anticipate difficulties instead. Then they isolate those difficulties and prepare contingencies. They find a way to deliver.

Great SMEs execute on a plan and find a way to do so repeatedly, reliably, and consistently.

101

SEEK PRODUCTIVITY

In its simplest form, productivity is determined by taking the value of goods or services produced and dividing it by the cost of production. Few experts know their own productivity. They might know subjectively how they are doing at their job, but they don't typically know quantitatively how their performance fulfills their organization's needs, nor do they know how their productivity compares with others.

I once worked with an information technology manager who believed his most important metric was the company's network reliability. He believed that his organization's network uptime was important above all else. Consequently, he spent an exorbitant amount of time and resources squeezing out the smallest possible vulnerabilities. He pursued double, triple, and quadruple redundancies to ensure service twenty-four seven. Cost management, it seemed, was a low and distant priority.

In reality, however, leaders in his organization were highly interested in cost management. Of course, the company needed reliable networks, but leadership did not value the network as highly as the IT manager, and they certainly did not believe the requisite cost was warranted. To the chief financial officer, the cost of a perfect network was not worth the investment required. This difference of opinion between the IT manager and the CFO boiled over and was never resolved.

Ultimately, the IT manager was replaced. His departure was not because he was poor at his job. To the contrary, he was an excellent technician and a skilled leader of his team. He was an expert in his field and his competency was rarely questioned. But he would not accept the metrics used to measure his performance. He overstated the value of a reliable network, and he refused to believe that his productivity was somehow tied to the cost of services he rendered.

By definition, productivity is always tied to value and cost. Therefore, experts who refuse to recognize the true value of their services and the full cost of those services do themselves and the people around them a disservice. Too many experts think they are the arbiters of their own productivity and value. They think that what they measure matters more than what others measure.

The best experts seek objective feedback. They want measurements that accurately reflect value and cost. They don't exaggerate their own value, and they don't deflate their own cost. They maximize true productivity by delivering the best possible version of goods and services at the best possible cost.

102

LESSONS FROM TENNIS

The record for the fastest tennis serve ever delivered in a professional match is 163 miles per hour by Sam Groth in 2012.[66] It is common for professional male players to deliver serves above 130 miles per hour. The task of returning a serve at that speed is beyond challenging; mathematically, it is impossible.

A tennis serve travels about seventy-five feet. When you take into consideration the bounce of the ball, air friction, and spin, it takes about seven hundred milliseconds for a ball to travel from one end of the court to the other. When you calculate the amount of time it takes the human eye and nervous system to process a ball's movement at that speed, and then consider the time required for a human body to move and accurately swing a racket, the return cannot be performed. The math doesn't add up. The human body can't process information and move fast enough to return a professional serve. It can't be done.[67]

This brings us to one important action that expert tennis players can do and which all SMEs should do. The greatest tennis players anticipate the ball's location. They use clues beyond the ball itself to predict the future. After thousands of hours of practice, the best tennis players can judge a server's initial toss, posture, and racket placement, and anticipate with accuracy the ball's eventual location.

Great experts learn to anticipate. They see clues in advance, which lesser mortals do not see. They do not rely solely on the path of the ball itself to tell them where the ball is going. Instead, they incorporate everything around the ball as well.

103

LESSONS FROM CHESS

Researchers have studied chess for centuries. Some of the earliest investigations into memory and problem-solving took place in this domain, and many of the greatest chess players in history have been the subjects of investigation and intrigue.

Scientists focus on chess for several reasons, not least of which is how easily these experts can be identified and measured. The top chess players in the world are ranked, and the skills of one chess player can easily be tested against the skills of another. No aspiring player can pretend they are better than they truly are for long. Furthermore, test environments are easily created.

Of course, chess is mostly a mental exercise. Competition does not favor a player's size, age, gender, race, education, language, or nationality. The eight-by-eight grid and thirty-two pieces are understood by millions of people but mastered by very few. A young child can learn the game in a few minutes, yet the masters remain obsessed for decades. Chess, it seems, is a researcher's playground.[68][69][70]

Entire books have been written about the lessons that experts can derive from the game of chess. Some educators recommend chess as a mandatory subject of study in public K–12 education. Space does not permit an exhaustive list of the game's merits for SMEs, but here are three that experts should think about.

First, contrary to popular belief, master chess players do not think many moves ahead of their competitors.[71] Instead, they see the relative strengths and weaknesses of groups, or chunks, of moves that can be choreographed together. This process of "chunking"[72] allows masters to see patterns in player positions and have mental templates or representations to guide effective moves.

Second, victory favors those with the more effective memory. Experts can look at a board and quickly remember, based on experience and study, what strategies will be effective given a certain configuration. The deeper the memory of comparable chess configurations, the greater the advantage.

Third, individual players can change the balance of power. Master chess players not only can see the strengths and weaknesses of board configurations, but they can also see how individual players can change the dynamics of the entire board through strategic adjustments. Unlike junior competitors, chess masters can see how repositioning one or two simple resources can change the entire balance of the match.[73]

All SMEs benefit when they see strategy in terms of patterns rather than individual moves and when they remember what worked in the past and how those experiences map to the present. And they all increase their effectiveness when they isolate and reposition individual assets that turn the tables and convert weak positions into strong ones.

104

EXPERTS ARE MEASURED

Major League Baseball players are some of the most highly measured experts in the world. They are evaluated publicly in hundreds of ways. They are scrutinized for virtually everything they do on the field, and many of their multimillion-dollar contracts contain incentives reflecting these metrics.

In offensive play, teams want to see home runs, bases on balls, and runs batted in. They don't want to see strikeouts, ground outs, or runners stranded.

Individual players in the game know how they are doing throughout the season. They know how their metrics compare to their teammates and their opponents. They are reminded frequently when they are doing well and when they are not. There is no hiding from the metrics that follow them. For good or bad, these statistics will dog them for the rest of their lives on league websites and collector baseball cards.

All organizations have productivity measurements. Few are as public as Major League Baseball, but all organizations track and measure performance. They compare their performance with competitors, industry norms, and projections. They do it for the benefit of the organization, its divisions, teams, and even for individuals.

As we previously discussed, experts should seek to understand their own productivity. Unlike professional baseball players, most experts have no idea how they are being measured. They have a general sense for how things are going, but they rarely know the specific metrics. They are like a professional baseball player who does not know his own batting average or who hasn't counted his own home runs.

Ironically, many of these same experts are emphatically scientific in other areas of their professions. They track the performance of their products, equipment, and services. They know how to measure almost everything except themselves.

Great experts understand and know how to measure their own performance. They know which of their performances are key to their success, which of their actions make a real difference, and how to measure the efficacy of those actions. Obviously, not all expert performances can be measured as easily as in Major League Baseball, but all expertise can be measured in some way and should be.

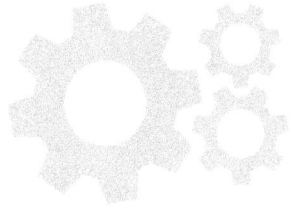

105

ENTHUSIASM

Few things are more agonizing than listening to a lifeless subject matter expert yammer about some technical subject that few people care about. SMEs should show energy and passion for their subject. They need to demonstrate with their posture and tone that they care. The legendary National Football League coach Vince Lombardi put it this way, "If you aren't fired with enthusiasm, you will be fired with enthusiasm."[74]

106

CONTROL EMOTIONS

Some experts spend considerable effort removing emotion from their empirically based work. Many experts think emotion is irrelevant to their expertise. They attempt to convince others of their informed viewpoint through antiseptically developed scientific methodology and statistically significant conclusions. But even the soundest reason has its limitations.

We often think people should control their emotions when they get excited, weepy, or angry, but we rarely suggest emotional control when someone is void of emotion. Western culture encourages emotionless interactions, and experts seem particularly inclined to oblige. Being emotionless may seem like the safest approach to professional interaction, but it is not the most effective. If you are not passionate about your subject, others will not be passionate about it either.

It is emotion, more than proof, that motivates a person to act on your words. It is emotion, more than statistics, that inspires, and it is emotion, more than probability, that reassures. The more you subtract emotion from your work, the less persuasive your arguments will become.

The best experts control their emotions. They are not hotheads, but they are also not stone-cold statues either. They intentionally insert emotion where appropriate to be most effective. Controlling emotion is not just a process of removing it. No, controlling emotion means you can turn it on and off to create and enhance your relationships of trust.

107

PATIENCE WITH
THE UNSKILLED

In 1995 McArthur Wheeler robbed two Pittsburgh banks in broad daylight and made his escape. Remarkably, he looked directly at multiple security cameras during the robberies with no attempt to cover his face. His picture was broadcast that evening on the eleven o'clock news, and he was arrested an hour later. Investigators later learned that Wheeler had rubbed lemon juice on his face and was under the impression that doing so would make him invisible to cameras. He reasoned that lemon juice can be used as an invisible ink on paper, so if he rubbed it on his entire face, he would become invisible to cameras. This stunning bit of ignorance is surprising but sadly not unusual.

Prompted by Wheeler's bank robbery, two researchers at Cornell University, David Dunning and Justin Kruger, began studying the accuracy of self-assessment. They wondered how people could be such poor judges of their own abilities. Their research was published in a 1999 report titled, "Unskilled and Unaware of It."

Now dubbed the Dunning-Kruger effect, the research explored an important concept that all experts should know and recognize. It is human nature for unskilled people to be horribly poor judges of their own ability. They fail to recognize their own lack of skill, and furthermore, they are poor judges of the skills of others. It is true across any discipline or industry. Whether we are talking about dancers, painters, sociologists, or mathematicians, the lowest quartile of performers has the most inflated opinion of their own ability.

This phenomenon can be particularly frustrating for experts. Time and again, you will encounter uneducated, untrained, or unskilled people who think, speak, and act as if they are proficient, when they clearly are not. Charles Darwin recognized this phenomenon when he penned, "Ignorance more frequently begets confidence than does knowledge."[75]

As an expert, you might prefer that the unskilled people around you recognize that they are unskilled. Unfortunately, this is not the case. Experts of all stripes should expect unskilled people to have inflated opinions of their own capability. It is simply the way it is. Yet too often experts are surprised and even aghast when they encounter the "unskilled and unaware."

Unfortunately, there is very little an expert can do to quickly reverse the Dunning-Kruger effect. Confronting the novice will not rectify an inflated perception. Telling the untrained that they are wrong more often fosters resentment than cooperation. Pointing out the failings of the beginner will not reduce their opinion of themself, but it will reduce their opinion of you.

There is one remedy for the Dunning-Kruger effect, but it takes time to accomplish. The better trained a person is at a task, the more proficient that person becomes, and the better judge they become of their own skill. Once a person becomes proficient at something, their perception of their skills becomes more accurate. They also gain an appreciation for the skill of the true expert.

The least-skilled people will still tend to hold the highest degree of illusory superiority, and moderately skilled individuals will still tend to maintain a higher opinion of themselves than is justified. So, don't be surprised when people are unskilled and unaware. It is only the truly proficient who underestimate their own abilities.

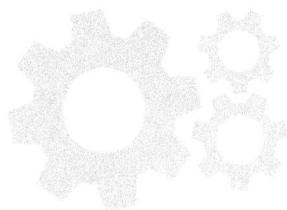

108

FAIL FAST

Venture capitalists hold the philosophy that if a business is going to fail, it should fail quickly. Slowly failing businesses are bad for customers, bad for employees, and particularly bad for investors. The faster something is shut down, the faster something better can take its place, and the faster everyone involved can concentrate on different and better innovations. In business, failing fast is almost always better than failing slowly.

There is merit to this idea beyond the realm of business ventures and financial investments. If an idea is bad, it will eventually fail. As an expert you want to know it is bad as quickly as possible. Delayed awareness that an idea is bad does not make the idea good. To the contrary, delayed awareness only increases the likelihood of failure and the magnitude of the damage.

People knew as far back as the 1800s that exposure to asbestos was bad for human health. Yet, because of its abundance and low cost, we used the material in thousands of products. Eventually, the mistake of using asbestos in these products became evident, but by then, it had become enormous. After decades of remediation, there are still thousands of people each year who die from asbestos exposure.

Bad ideas are eventually uncovered. Ironically, experts often suspect failures far before they occur. Great experts can reveal bad ideas faster than anyone else. To do this, they need to remove all rose-colored glasses and vigilantly ask themselves and others probing questions. When will this idea fail? What circumstances will cause this theory to collapse? Why is this idea better than the next best alternative?

When you do find flaws in ideas, your role as an SME is not complete. Far from it. Fault-finding is not your sole objective. If you spend all your time pointing out the failings of ideas without offering solutions, you will quickly become an unpopular expert, and with good reason. Finding a flaw is the beginning of your job, not the end. Far too many experts believe their sole responsibility is to approve or reject the recommendations of others. To the contrary, an expert's higher responsibility is to improve on the recommendations of others and find ways to solve problems.

If an idea's failure is inevitable, then your job as an expert is to make it known quickly, accurately, and convincingly. Never allow your company, your friends, your colleagues, or your customers to drive off a cliff while you watch from the bleachers. If problems can be fixed, then fix them. If you can't fix them yourself, then quickly recommend corrections to people who can fix them. If something is going to fail, then you should ensure it fails fast.

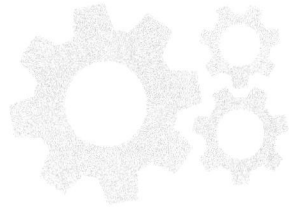

109

FAIL CHEAPLY

Failing cheaply is a close sibling to failing fast. Experts should spend as little money and time as possible on exposing bad ideas. Don't spend two dollars proving something is wrong if you can prove it for one dollar instead. Don't spend two hours researching a bad idea if one hour will do. Bad ideas don't deserve your time, money, or emotional energy.

Bad ideas are like abusive relationships. No matter how much you hope an idea will yield happiness, a bad idea is certain to bring disappointment or despair. Bad ideas also will appear attractive and charming at first, but they end up sucking the energy out of everything you do. Bad ideas should be jettisoned as quickly as possible with as little cost as possible. If you are going to fail, then do it fast and do it cheaply.

110

BE PREPARED

The Boy Scouts' motto is Be Prepared, and the US Coast Guard's motto is Semper Paratus, or Always Ready. These short phrases encapsulate an idea that should guide all of us, both personally and professionally.

Life was not simple for the Baker family. Sharon Baker had been abandoned by her husband many years earlier and was left to raise her daughter and three boys alone. Her children were about the same age as my children, and our families became friends. With her permission, I would like to share her experience with you.

I remember the day when thieves broke into their home and stole many of her family's belongings. I also remember the day when Sharon's ex-husband unexpectedly passed away and the mixed feelings her children experienced. They had not seen their father in more than a decade and he had never provided support, yet he was still their father and now he was dead.

One day, I received a telephone call from a mutual friend who informed me that Sharon had lost her job. I worried about this fine family and felt some duty to help them. I knew that Sharon would not easily accept assistance. Nevertheless, within a few days, I visited the Baker home with the intention of providing financial assistance. When I arrived, Sharon greeted me warmly. After some brief pleasantries and an acknowledgment of her job situation, I became assertive, maybe more than ever before.

"Sharon," I asked, "do you have sufficient food?"

"Yes," she replied.

"Is your rent current?" I asked.

"Yes."

"It is cold outside—are your heating and electric bills paid?"

"Yes."

"How much fuel is in your vehicle?"

"I have plenty of gas."

"Do the children have winter clothes?"

"Yes."

Finally, she stopped me and said something like this: "Alan, I was taught by my parents and many other fine people to be prepared, to stay out of debt, to live within my means, and to save a little money. For years this is what I have done. We have everything we need. We will be fine."

I went to Sharon's home with the intention of helping her, yet through her commitment to sound principles, she lifted me.

It is unfortunate how much we ignore preparation for stormy times or unexpected events. Great experts, however, are prepared. Great experts expect circumstances to change. They operate within their means, they prepare for the risks around them, and they protect their constituents from the storms that inevitably come. Oh, that all experts could be as wise and prepared as that single mother!

111

KNOW THE LAWS

All experts should understand the laws that govern their discipline. Don't abide in ignorance. One of the fastest ways to lose credibility as an expert is to demonstrate ignorance of the laws that govern you. You should know the legislative and case laws, how they came to be, and who participated in the creation of the laws.

Too many experts get their first experience with the legal system when they are subpoenaed to appear in court. Ask any such expert if closer attention to legal matters in advance would have been helpful. Learn from those who have been embroiled in drawn-out legal battles. Learn the legal constructs in advance and be prepared to answer for your actions.

In addition to the law, you should understand the legal pitfalls of your discipline and be well-versed in risk avoidance. It is impossible to guarantee that someone will never be sued, but you can understand where the biggest risks are and how to avoid violations.

Always be vigilant about legal matters. Remain prepared for the worst possible legal situation. Keep notes and stay well within the laws to avoid even the appearance of impropriety.

Despite the legal minefields, don't become paralyzed by risk. We enter a legal system every time we start the engine of our vehicle. Negligence behind the wheel can result in death or imprisonment. Knowing that fact should not paralyze drivers into inaction. You should understand the dangers and remain confident in your ability to manage those dangers.

112

MEDIATOR

A mediator is a person who helps settle disputes between parties. Synonyms for mediator include advocate, judge, and arbiter. One of the primary roles of an SME is to find common ground between multiple parties. SMEs don't just recommend solutions to satisfy the dominant decision maker; they identify a way forward that benefits everyone.

As discussed earlier, experts see things that other people do not. They also "chunk" information into different and unique autonomous units. They see more possibilities, process the possibilities more quickly, and identify the best alternatives more efficiently and accurately than other people. Consequently, experts are ideally suited for mediation. They understand the perspectives of contradictory points of view and quickly move to satisfy all parties.

Mediators don't pick sides. They may be assigned to a side by virtue of employment, association, or historical factors, but they must remain neutral and objective. They find mutually beneficial paths with the least cost, the least effort, the least risk, and the least disruption. They reveal a path to give both sides what they want, rather than what they don't want.

113

DON'T SCAPEGOAT

I n ancient times, there were small communities of people who would select young goats from their herds, blame the goats for the sins of the people, and banish the goats to the wilderness to carry away these transgressions. The scapegoat, as it came to be known, is the bearer of responsibility, the one who is falsely blamed for transgressions.

It is an appealing concept that someone else can take the blame and burden for another, so much so that scapegoating has occurred throughout recorded history. Adam blamed Eve for partaking of the forbidden fruit. In Greek mythology, Pandora is responsible for opening the box that unleashed all human trouble. There seems to be a universal instinct to blame other people for our own actions. Scapegoating is as prevalent today as ever. We may not banish goats into the wilderness or sacrifice them on altars, but we do have a propensity to allocate blame. When things go wrong many people will say it was their colleague's fault, or their subordinate's fault, or their boss's fault, or their customer's fault. When someone else can be blamed, many people look to do that first.

Great SMEs resist the temptation to blame. They know that scapegoating is unbecoming of an expert. It diminishes credibility and corrodes trust. If an SME correctly blames someone nine times out of ten, the audience will still remember the one time when the SME assigned blame erroneously. Great

SMEs take responsibility for errors. They assume a mistake was their own until they are completely certain that the problem lies someplace else. Even when a problem is not the SME's responsibility, they do what they can to alleviate the burden on the responsible party. It is never enough to point a finger and walk away. Great SMEs quickly and accurately identify the real sources of problems and then cooperate in the solution. They know blaming never solves anything.

114

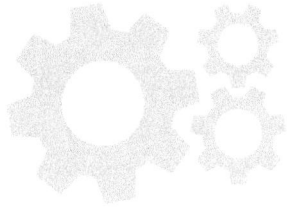

BE SLOW TO CORRECT

A few years ago, a colleague asked me, "What's the best way to correct someone when they're wrong?" The answer depends on what you are trying to accomplish. If an SME is only interested in being right, then the best correction is, well, no correction at all. It's almost always a bad idea to correct people. SMEs should do it rarely, which means almost never.

Just because people get things wrong doesn't mean SMEs should jump in with corrections; doing so is typically counterproductive. The question asked by my colleague smacks of arrogance and condescension. He may as well have asked me, "What's the best way to correct someone when they're wrong and I'm right?" After all, that is what he was implying. Sadly, some SMEs feel the need to correct every falsehood and remedy every misconception. The counsel I offered my colleague was simple: "Don't correct people. Don't do it. Don't do it. Don't do it!"

It's not the duty of an SME to correct people. As mentioned previously, the duty of an SME is to build trust, establish mutual vision, and ensure delivery. Rarely do corrections contribute to those essential goals, and if a correction does not advance any of those three objectives, then there's a good chance it is motivated only by the pride and arrogance of the SME. Once again, don't do it.

On those rare instances when a correction is warranted, there are three important ingredients that it should include. First, if you must correct someone, you should enlighten rather than condemn. Your correction should reveal knowledge, light, and truth. It should increase people's confidence and broaden their perspective. Corrections from SMEs should lift, not diminish, and complement, not condemn.

Obviously, corrections are prevalent in certain professions. Teachers and coaches are expected to correct their pupils. Students cannot improve if they do not obtain corrective feedback from experts. But an SME must be motivated by love for their student, not by any arrogance or sense of superiority.

Second, your correction should be concise and actionable. The person being corrected should be crystal clear about what is wrong and how they can fix it. If the SME is not clear about what is wrong and how the error can be remedied, then there is little the other person can do with the correction. Sometimes just knowing something is wrong is better than not knowing, even if you don't know what to do about it. But your words as an SME will be much more effective if you can be concise about the problem and actionable about the solution.

We should also note that there is a difference between correcting people's ideas and correcting their actions. Actions follow ideas. When someone's behavior is in error, it is usually because they hold the wrong ideas. So, corrections should focus on ideas before behavior. It is more effective to correct the ideas that govern behavior than it is to correct the behavior itself. Teaching correct ideas will do more to change behavior than just focusing on the behavior. So, first correct the ideas. Then, if necessary, address the actions.

Finally, an SME's correction should be followed by an increased measure of empathy and support for the person who was corrected. People who are corrected, especially unexpectedly, will react negatively. Many will resent it and brand you as their enemy. Consequently, it is wise to prove otherwise. We live in a time when being told you are wrong is interpreted as being told you are stupid. Show the people you correct that you like them, that you care for them, and that your actions are in their best interest.

As a caveat, it is worth pointing out that corrections will be more effective if they come from an SME who has moral authority. If your life is consistent with your own advice, then you will be believable. No one likes a hypocrite. If people know you won't accept your own criticism, then your guidance will be in vain.

In conclusion, don't correct people unless you must. Do it only if it adds to trust, vision, or delivery. On the rare occasions that you do correct someone, lift them up, be clear and actionable, and follow with empathy and support—and do it from a position of moral authority. But most of all: Don't correct people. Don't do it. Don't do it. Don't do it!

115

ANECDOTE: CORRECTING

Many years ago, I was assigned to teach a class for my employer. After discussing the agenda with my boss, we decided to include one of my subordinates, Chuck, as an instructor. Chuck was fluent in the technology we would teach, and he would benefit from the process of preparing and teaching a portion of the class. My only reservation was that Chuck was difficult. To be honest, he was a jerk. He insisted on always being right and could offend nearly everyone in his path. Despite his impossible personality, however, he was a skilled technician. He could solve difficult problems and was respected by the company's technical leaders. But putting him in front of an entire class would be risky; he would almost certainly offend someone.

On the day of the class, I hoped for the best, but my worst fears were realized. Rather than bridling his worst impulses, Chuck's nerves seemed to amplify his displays of self-importance. He was self-righteous, arrogant, and condescending. I remember him responding to a student, "Are you asking me what Bash is? Are you serious? Does anybody else actually not know what Bash is?" I was horrified.

When the meeting ended, I was angry with Chuck and disappointed with myself for letting him teach. I asked Chuck to join me in my office to talk about the experience. My impulse was to correct Chuck harshly, but I held back. Instead, I simply asked, "How do you think the class went? How did we do?"

His response was immediate: "Not very well."

"Why?" I responded, relieved that he probably recognized just how poorly he had performed and what a jerk he was.

"Well, Alan, you did awful." He then started telling me all the ways I had done a poor job of teaching.

I was furious but I listened. It was difficult to listen, but somehow, I did. He told me I missed key items, that I moved through the material too slowly, and that I wasted time on simple questions. He went on and on. He didn't just talk about our experience that day. He talked about other situations as well. He talked about how I led meetings, how I communicated with customers, and how I made decisions. In retrospect, I am still surprised I had the patience for his corrections.

When Chuck finished, I said, "OK, Chuck, thanks for your feedback. What can I do to be a better instructor?" This gave Chuck the opportunity to repeat his criticisms, vent his frustrations, and tell me what I should be doing differently. To my disgust, he made some valid recommendations.

And then a miracle occurred. Chuck asked me, "Alan, now what do you think I could do to improve?" The question was entirely uncharacteristic. In the year that I had worked with him, I had never seen him express an openness to correction, not once. I could have told him a hundred things he was doing wrong, but I elected not to. Instead, I took the time to tell Chuck about several things he did well. I complimented his knowledge of the material and his high expectations for himself and others. I finally decided to correct him on just one thing. I said, "Chuck, I was puzzled by your reaction when someone said they don't know Bash. It felt a bit harsh." We then talked for a few minutes about the principle of kindness and how it applies even to great technicians. We then jointly committed to do better: me when giving instruction and Chuck in his reaction to coworkers. We agreed that we both had things to improve on.

After that experience I saw faint expressions of kindness from Chuck. The change was slight and he still offended people, but he became easier to work with. He learned that he could be kind.

A few months later I was transferred to another area of the company. I would occasionally hear from colleagues about Chuck's interaction with new leaders. I knew he was struggling. Eventually, I heard that he was leaving the company. I contacted him and took him out to lunch.

Afterward, I drove him back to his office. We sat in my car and Chuck said, "I hate this place. I can't wait to get out of here."

"I am sorry," I responded.

"For years now," he continued, "I've been told over and over what an awful engineer I am. Over and over people tell me I do this wrong or that wrong, or something else wrong. All from people who are too stupid to do anything right themselves. I hate it. The only boss who didn't correct me all the time was you."

"I am sorry," I said again. "I'm sure you've had far better bosses."

"No," he snapped. "Do you remember the time we taught that class together and you asked me what we could do to improve?"

"Yes, I remember."

"That was the only time in my years here that anyone has ever talked with me like that."

I was sad to hear him say that. He fought back a tear, shook my hand, opened the door, and returned to his office. He departed the company a few days later. I never saw him again.

116

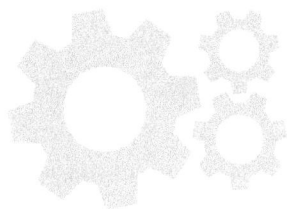

CLEAN UP MESSES

On October 21, 2013, President Barack Obama entered the Rose Garden and spent nearly an hour apologizing to the American people for the launch of HealthCare.gov. The insurance website designed by the federal government to allow consumers to purchase health insurance policies as mandated by the Affordable Care Act (ACA), aka Obamacare, was broken. "The website," President Obama said, "is not working the way it should."[76]

The website launch had quickly become a train wreck and threatened to upend the ACA, one of President Obama's crowning accomplishments. In response, the government engaged some of the world's finest information technology experts to fix the system and restore confidence. The new team quickly established a plan for solving the mess.

Experts are often called in to clean up other people's messes. It should be an honor to be entrusted with such a task. In the case of the HealthCare.gov issues, the measures the IT experts took are instructive to all experts who are called upon to fix other people's problems. Here are some tips for what SMEs should do in this situation.

Identify the true problems independent of politics, preferences, finger-pointing, and emotion. What is the actual problem, and more important, what precisely constitutes resolution of the problem?

Identify the obstacles to resolution. There will always be barriers to fixing a problem. The expert must be empowered to perform the work required. If the necessary actions cannot be taken, then the problem will not be solved.

Include the people who understand the problem and want to fix it. An expert can rarely walk into a critical problem when tension is high and solve the problem without the contribution of those who have been involved from the beginning.

Avoid blame. Finger-pointing was plentiful in the days immediately after the launch of HealthCare.gov. Republicans blamed the Democrats, government bureaucrats blamed the contractors, and so on. Ultimately, the people who solved the problem ignored the blame game and focused on the problems and solutions, not any incompetence or malevolence.

Don't jump to conclusions. Even if you think you know what is wrong and how to solve it, don't embrace a solution until all other possibilities are eliminated.

Involve people with knowledge, not rank. Just because a person appears at the top of the org chart or sits in a corner office does not mean they know what is wrong. Cubicles hold solutions just as readily as offices do.

Focus. Triage the immediate problems and resolve them first. Organize all remaining issues and prioritize them for resolution.

Whether you love or hate Obamacare, the fact is the website launch was resolved. The right people came together and fixed the problems that ailed the initial launch. Enrollments went from twenty-six thousand to nearly one million in one month.

117

KNOW THE FULL COST

There is always a cost for obtaining the services of an expert. Even on the odd occasion when an expert provides services pro bono, there are many other costs linked to the situation. Customers need to find a qualified expert and then they need to fully describe the services they need. They often have to wait for the expert to provide a recommendation and then validate it. Once customers accept the advice of an expert, they often need to negotiate the terms of further engagements. This entire process takes time, money, and attention. Throughout the entire process, the customer could have been doing other valuable things instead.

Remember, people who pay for your expertise are paying with more than money. They are paying with their time and attention. They may be betting their very future based on your recommendations. The best experts understand that the total cost of obtaining their services is far higher than the price tag on the invoice.

As an SME, your expertise is often only one part of an overall project. Most of the time your skills alone are insufficient to accomplish what the customer needs. Your services provide value, but only when orchestrated with a host of other experts, professionals, assets, and resources. So, as you consider the true cost of delivering your expertise, be careful to keep that expertise in the context of the overall solution. It probably takes more than just you to deliver the solution and to continue realizing benefits from the solution. Yours is not the only cost. Keep your contribution in the appropriate context and your cost as one important component of a more costly solution.

118

ATTRIBUTE SUCCESS

Great experts don't pat themselves on the back or take credit when things go well. They give credit to others sincerely and generously.

In Super Bowl LIII, the New England Patriots beat the Los Angeles Rams 13–3. After the game, Patriots' coach Bill Belichick was called the best coach of all time.[77] Instead of accepting credit for himself, he immediately gave credit to the players. He said, "This is a great day for our football team. Obviously, Mr. Kraft [the team owner] put this all together, but it's all about the players. These guys worked so hard all year. They just competed every week. And they competed today like champions. They played like champions."[78]

When pressed further to take credit, he was asked, "How did you come up with a game plan like that to stop the Rams?"

To which Belichick responded, "Well, it's tough. They're a great football team. They're very well coached, but it's really about the players. They made the plays. They stopped the run. They tackled the quarterback. They covered the receivers."[79]

Two years later, Tom Brady, the longtime quarterback under Belichick, moved to the Tampa Bay Buccaneers. This time, in Super Bowl LV, Brady won the championship, again. With the focus on Brady, he too pointed to his teammates: "I'm so proud of all these guys out here."[80] Buccaneers head coach

Bruce Arians added, "This really belongs to our coaching staff and our players. I didn't do a thing. You guys won this game."

All SMEs can take a lesson from these football experts. No matter how much credit you deserve for your part in a victory, you can always extend the credit to others. Few SMEs are successful alone.

119

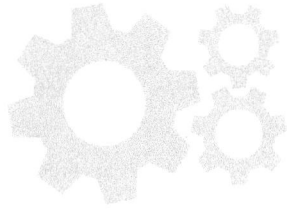

FILTERING PROSPECTS

Part of ensuring delivery on the part of an SME involves filtering bad situations in advance. Not all customers are good for business. Many customers drain the energy out of an organization through complaints, product enhancement requests, scheduling expectations, tight margins, and low morale. But eliminating bad customers can be difficult, especially after a contract is negotiated and work begins. So, SMEs are occasionally tasked with the responsibility of identifying bad customers before it's too late. Better that an SME identify and eliminate counterproductive customers at the outset, than to start a relationship and be forced to unravel it under negative terms. Better to cancel a wedding than negotiate a divorce.

All employees involved in the selling process have a responsibility to identify and eliminate bad customers. SMEs, however, are uniquely suited to be gatekeepers and goaltenders for their organizations.

The typical sales representative is tasked with identifying and adding top-line revenue, not removing it. Corporate leadership and sales management might say they don't want bad customers, but truthfully, sales representatives are rarely incentivized to reduce top-line revenue even if that reduction will improve their company's margin. Sales representatives are encouraged to think about revenue growth far more than operating efficiency.

SMEs, on the other hand, are not faced with the same mandate. They are responsible for trust, vision, and delivery, so that means they can see the customer through the lens of mutual viability. SMEs must know the customer's expectations and must be confident that those expectations can be met and exceeded.

So, when SMEs become involved in the process of bringing new customers on board, they must consider all customer expectations, those contractually defined and otherwise. If we engage with this customer, what do they expect? Which expectations are most important? If an expectation cannot be satisfied, then what alternatives are available? When must each expectation be satisfied? How much effort is required to do it?

When an SME does identify a potential mismatch between the customer's expectations and the company's ability to deliver, it is incumbent upon the SME to bring the mismatch to the attention of their team. SMEs should not attempt to reject a potential customer relationship unilaterally. The decision to add a customer is always made in consultation with others.

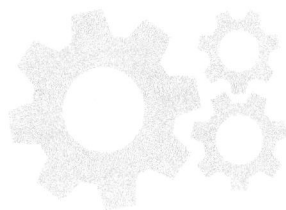

120

COERCION

Early in my career I was assigned to create a website for a major client. As far as I knew, this would be the first online vehicle ordering system in the automotive industry. At the time, I was young and had limited experience leading large projects; nevertheless, I was given the task and entrusted with a large budget.

One key piece of the project was acquiring the computer equipment to host the service. For assistance I consulted with the experts at a well-known hardware manufacturer, which was a preferred vendor to my client. The manufacturer made an aggressive recommendation that my engineering team and I thought was expensive. We challenged the vendor, but its SMEs responded with haughtiness and condescension. We went ahead and accepted their recommendation and made the large purchase.

When the website was launched a few months later, we learned that the equipment did not match our needs. We had purchased far more gear than was necessary, only confirming our suspicions about the proposal. The vendor had taken advantage of a well-funded project and my lack of experience.

Fortunately, we were able to reallocate some of the equipment to other projects and eventually grow into the remaining servers. Within twelve months, the excess capacity was properly allocated. The website was a big success for me, my teammates, and the client.

There was one loser in the project. Because of the behavior of the vendor's SMEs during the project, they gained a reputation for being scammers and blowhards. They became known as exaggerators at best and liars at worst. They lost their ongoing relationship with the company, and because of that they lost out on other large equipment purchases. They secured one large sale on my project but lost far more business going forward.

Experts can feel pressured or tempted to exaggerate at times. This might manifest as overstating the size or complexity of a problem, overplaying the effort required to complete a task, or overstating the skills needed to resolve a problem. An SME might be incentivized to propose a larger sale than is prudent. Regardless of the circumstances, effective SMEs don't coerce the customer. They don't apply undo pressure on clients to do what they themselves would not do.

121

REVEAL YOUR PREFERENCES

Few people are truly impartial. Some people prefer soup; others like salad. Some people like the window seat; others like the aisle. Some people enjoy rollercoasters; others are afraid of them. Experts, like everyone else, are influenced by their experience, education, colleagues, and more. And personal feelings, expectations, and aspirations frequently color what they say and do.

Experts have plenty of preferences, especially within their specialty. The more an expert learns about a subject, the more that expert becomes partial to specific techniques, processes, tools, and metrics. Often, the more expertise a person acquires, the more steeped with preferences they become.

People expect experts to possess bias. They rightly doubt that experts can become proficient without developing biases. As an SME, your audience believes you are biased, and with rare exceptions, they are correct. Therefore, you do not serve yourself, your audience, or your company well by hiding your preferences or pretending they do not exist. The best experts know they possess a certain perspective. They acknowledge that perspective and speak objectively about it. They distinguish preferences that matter from those that do not. Great experts don't stubbornly hold onto preferences for the sake of habit, manipulation, or control. They quickly reject their own preferences when superior alternatives are discovered, and they regularly look for opportunities to change.

Some experts mistakenly believe that they sound more trustworthy, credible, or wise if they hide their preferences or deny they exist. For example, they think it is somehow inappropriate to boldly promote their own company's products or services. They feel that their qualifications as an expert require them to be purely objective and totally impartial, even to the extent of denying their own motives or financial incentives.

SMEs should be big enough to admit where their preferences lie. If an SME's compensation is attached in any way to a product or service within their domain, then they cannot be neutral. So, as an SME, don't even try to be unbiased. If you portray yourself as unbiased, you are not believable. Pretending to be objective when you are not is damaging. Unapologetic objectivity is liberating to everyone.

CONCLUSION

CONCLUSION

D r. Anthony Fauci was thrust into the public spotlight when President Trump announced the White House Coronavirus Task Force in January 2020.[81] He quickly became the nation's leading public expert on COVID-19. Prior to the pandemic, Fauci had worked as the director of the National Institute of Allergy and Infectious Diseases for decades. He was a highly accomplished medical professional, advisor to multiple US presidents, and winner of the Presidential Medal of Freedom. But, like most experts, he was mostly unknown to the American public. Within a few months of his introduction, however, he had been interviewed hundreds of times and lauded by major news sources for his important role in fighting the disease. Now he is recognized by hundreds of millions of Americans.

Some people speak his name with honor and respect, for instance *The New Yorker* dubbed Fauci "America's Doctor."[82] Others express scorn, such as when *The Wall Street Journal* said, "Dr. Anthony Fauci has proven he doesn't understand economics . . . [or] public health."[83]

Being a public expert is not easy. It is fraught with trials, criticism, and difficulty, but we need these experts, sometimes desperately. We impulsively seek experts at times of risk, trial, and uncertainty. We expect experts to fix what ails our companies, our relationships, our health, and our psychology.

We expect experts to protect us from stupidity and harm. We expect experts to know, predict, and shape the future. We blame them when things go wrong.

In January 2020 Fauci could not possibly have known the full impact of COVID-19 on American health, much less the full impact on our economics, politics, and culture. The best he could do under the circumstance is the same thing that any other expert can do, namely:

Confront and overcome the challenges. The volume and diversity of information and technology are accelerating, making expertise more difficult than ever. Experts have less time to convince their audience, they are thinly sliced, and they are being confronted by endless distractions in their quest for influence. Experts are surrounded by fakers and naysayers. They are either noticed, scrutinized, and criticized, or completely ignored. Great SMEs confront challenges directly. They know they must in order for their influence to be established, felt, and maintained.

Continually seek knowledge and skill. It is not enough for experts to be good at what they do. They must be exceptional. The day you deliberately stop practicing is the day you start backsliding. You must continually gather and filter new information, new research, new solutions, and newly discovered failures. By staying within your expert domain, you are less likely to lead people astray or make critical errors. You must be confident, resolute, and steadfast in the things you know to be right and appropriately cautionary in the things that are wrong.

Establish trust. Without trust, experts have nothing, so great SMEs work diligently to establish relationships of trust. They know that trust is built on superior knowledge and skill as well as pure motive. They demonstrate what they believe through their behavior and they spend their time where it is most effective. Great experts don't use technical jargon. They don't condescend, scare, or criticize their audience. They avoid saying no and they find ways to say yes.

Determine a mutual vision. Great SMEs learn what their audience expects. They separate what is wanted from what is needed, and they simplify everything that is not reduced to its fundamental elements. The ignore nothing and no one. They teach what is enduring and sound with clarity and precision. They maintain temperance and express malice toward none.

Ensure delivery. They always find a way to deliver the goods, the solution, the cure. Love him or not, Anthony Fauci will always be able to point to Operation Warp Speed as the fastest vaccine development in human history. Experts in the federal government and the private sector created effective vaccines for COVID-19 in less than a year. Great experts seek productivity improvements, they measure their progress, and they know and influence the laws that govern them. Great experts deliver solutions.

After decades of observation, study, and research, I commend these principles to you. We need more experts, and we need better experts. Our products and services are increasing in sophistication and complexity. Our problems are getting bigger and more challenging. Our world is filled with pain and problems, contests and contention. Many things need to be changed and improved, and many people need assistance. The world is rarely changed by the ordinary, the good enough, or the commonplace. No, changing the world requires experts—people with tremendous capacity, tenacity, strength, and courage. Experts can make a profound difference in the world and they *should* make a profound difference in the world.

Together, let's advance the cause and the influence of the experts.

REFERENCES

CHB: Anders Ericsson, Robert R. Hoffman, Aaron Kozbelt, and A. Mark Williams, *The Cambridge Handbook of Expertise and Expert Performance*, 2nd Edition (Cambridge University Press, 2018).

PEAK: Anders Ericsson and Robert Pool, *Peak: Secrets from the New Science of Expertise* (Boston: Houghton Mifflin Harcourt, 2016).

SE: David Z. Hambrick, Guillermo Campitelli, and Brooke N. Macnamara, *The Science of Expertise: Behavioral, Neural, and Genetic Approaches to Complex Skills* (New York: Routledge, 2018).

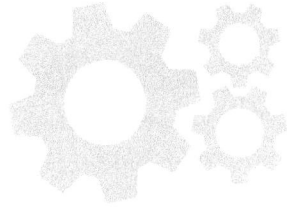

NOTES

1. CHB, 3–4.

2. CHB, 4.

3. SE, 39. See also Giovanni Sala and Fernand Gobet, *Do the Benefits of Chess Instruction Transfer to Academic and Cognitive Skills? A Meta-Analysis* (Educational Research Review, 2016).

4. David Epstein, *Range: Why Generalists Triumph in a Specialized World* (New York: Riverhead Books, 2019).

5. Emmie Martin, "Alex Rodriguez Shares His Best Advice for Young Entrepreneurs," Yahoo! Finance, June 15, 2017, https://sg.finance.yahoo.com/news/alex-rodriguez-shares-best-advice-121500142.html.

6. Zameena Mejia, "Why Oprah Winfrey Loves Malcolm Gladwell's Idea That Putting in 10,000 Hours Is Key to Success," CNBC, July 9, 2018, https://www.cnbc.com/2018/07/09/oprah-winfrey-loves-the-malcolm-gladwell-10000-hours-rule.html.

7. PEAK, 112.

8. SE, 154.

9. Ralph W. Stacy, *Computers in Biomedical Research* (1965) 320.

10. Marie Brown and Jennifer Bussell, "Medication Adherence: WHO Cares?" Mayo Clinic, 2011, www.ncbi.nlm.nih.gov/pmc/articles/PMC3068890.

11. World Health Organization, *Adherence to Long-Term Therapies: Evidence for Action* (World Health Organization, 2003) 30, http://www.who.int/chp/knowledge/publications/adherence_full_report.pdf.

12. Jane Ogden, Kaz Fuks, Mary Gardner, Steve Johnson, Malcolm McLean, Pam Martin, Reena Shah, "Doctors Expressions of Uncertainty and Patient Confidence," Patient Education and Counseling, 48, no. 2 (Oct.–Nov. 2002): 171–176.

13. Stuart Oskamp, "Overconfidence in Case-Study Judgments," *Journal of Consulting Psychology* (1965): 261–265.

14. Colin Camerer, George Loewenstein, and Martin Weber, "The Curse of Knowledge in Economic Settings: An Experimental Analysis," *Journal of Political Economy*, 97, no. 5 (October 1989).

15. Steven Pinker, *The Sense of Style: The Thinking Person's Guide to Writing in the 21st Century* (New York: Penguin Books, 2015) 57–76.

16. Nick Gass, "Trump: 'The Experts Are Terrible,'" Politico, April 4, 2016, https://www.politico.com/blogs/2016-gop-primary-live-updates-and-results/2016/04/donald-trump-foreign-policy-experts-221528.

17. Tom Nichols, *The Death of Expertise: The Campaign against Established Knowledge and Why It Matters* (New York: Oxford University Press, 2017) 3.

18. Nancy LeTourneau, "The 'Swamp' Trump Is Draining: Expertise," *Washington Monthly*, August 9, 2019, https://washingtonmonthly.com/2019/08/09/the-swamp-trump-is-draining-expertise.

19. Eltjo Buringh and Jan Luiten van Zanden, "Charting the Rise of the West: Manuscripts and Printed Books in Europe, A Long-Term Perspective from the Sixth through Eighteenth Centuries," *The Journal of Economic History* (2009) 409–445.

20. Nathaniel Branden, *Judgment Day: My Years with Ayn Rand* (New York: Houghton Mifflin, 1989).

21. William Shakespeare, *As You Like It* (1623).

22. Elliott Krause, *Death of the Guilds: Professions, States and the Advance of Capitalism, 1930 to the Present* (New Haven, CT: Yale University Press, 1999).

23. Kathryn Schulz, *Being Wrong: Adventures in the Margin of Error* (New York: HarperCollins, 2010) 5.

24. Nichols, *The Death of Expertise*, 196.

25. Jeremy Heimans and Henry Timms, "Understanding 'New Power,'" *Harvard Business Review*, December 2014, https://hbr.org/2014/12/understanding-new-power.

NOTES

26. CHB, 45.

27. Rosemarie Jarski, *Words from the Wise: Over 6,000 of the Smartest Things Ever Said* (Skyhorse Publishing, 2007) 170.

28. Nalini Ambady and Robert Rosenthal, "Half a Minute: Predicting Teacher Evaluations from Thin Slices of Nonverbal Behavior and Physical Attractiveness," *Journal of Personality and Social Psychology* (1993): 431–441, http://dx.doi.org/10.1037/0022-3514.64.3.431.

29. Nalini Ambady and Robert Rosenthal, "Thin Slices of Expressive Behavior as Predictors of Interpersonal Consequences: A Meta-Analysis," *Psychological Bulletin*, 111 (March 1992): 256–274, https://psycnet.apa.org/buy/1992-19793-001.

30. Henry Eyring, *Mormon Scientist: The Life and Faith of Henry Eyring* (Deseret Book Company, 2016) 194–195.

31. Richard Feynman, "Report of the Presidential Commission on the Space Shuttle Challenger Accident," NASA, February 11, 1986, https://history.nasa.gov/rogersrep/v4part4.htm; https://www.youtube.com/watch?v=ZOzoLdfWyKw.

32. Richard Branson's Blog, Virgin (website), https://www.virgin.com/branson-family/richard-branson-blog.

33. CBH, 35.

34. CBH, 127–148.

35. "Eugenics," History.com, A&E Television Networks, November 15, 2017, https://www.history.com/topics/germany/eugenics.

36. SE, 87–100.

37. "Anders Ericsson, Psychologist and 'Expert on Experts,' Dies at 72," *The New York Times*, July 1, 2020, https://www.nytimes.com/2020/07/01/science/anders-ericsson-dead.html.

38. SE, 152.

39. PEAK, 222–223.

40. Joseph Baker and Nick Wattie, "Innate Talent in Sport: Separating Myth from Reality," *Current Issues in Sport Science* (May 3, 2019).

41. SE, xiv.

42. CHB, 35.

43. Abraham Maslow, "A Theory of Human Motivation," *Psychological Review* 50 (1943): 370–396, http://psychclassics.yorku.ca/Maslow/motivation.htm.

245

44. PEAK, 98-100.

45. "The Democratic Debate in New Hampshire," *The New York Times*, January 5, 2008, https://www.nytimes.com/2008/01/05/us/politics/05text-ddebate.html.

46. Frank Dikötter, "Mao's Great Leap to Famine," *International Herald Tribune*, December 15, 2010.

47. "Table 2.2 Number of people affected by the Chernobyl accident (to December 2000)" (PDF), *The Human Consequences of the Chernobyl Nuclear Accident*. UNDP and UNICEF, January 22, 2002, p. 32; retrieved September 17, 2010.

48. "Halifax Explosion," Wikipedia, https://en.wikipedia.org/wiki/Halifax_Explosion.

49. Plato, *Protagoras*, trans. C.C.W. Taylor (Oxford: Clarendon Press, 1991).

50. Commercial featuring Charles Barkley, Nike (1993), https://www.youtube.com/watch?v=4gqk4WPnrpM.

51. CHB, 59–77.

52. GrumpyPenguin, "Do you consider yourselves like the 'Condescending Unix User?'" Reddit, March 17, 2014, https://www.reddit.com/r/sysadmin/comments/20lsod/do_you_consider_yourselves_like_the_condescending.

53. Nichols, *The Death of Expertise*, 64.

54. Marcia Angell, "Dispassionate Scientific Experts Would Benefit Courts," *The New York Times*, December 13, 1998.

55. Myra Ferree, William Gamson, Jürgen Gerhards, and Dieter Rucht, "Abortion Discourse: Democracy and Public Sphere in Germany and the United States," *American Journal of Sociology* (November 2004): 208.

56. Todd Nordstrom, "5 Reasons Being Passionate at Work Is Dangerous," Inc.com, November 28, 2017.

57. Frank Herron, "Never Never Never Give Up on Context for a Quotation," UMass Boston (blog), https://blogs.umb.edu/quoteunquote/2014/05/21/never-never-never-give-up-on-context-for-a-quotation.

58. Sigmund Freud, *Fragment of an Analysis of a Case of Hysteria* (1905) 1414, https://en.wikiquote.org/wiki/Sigmund_Freud.

59. Clayton Critcher and Melisa Ferguson, "The Cost of Keeping It Hidden: Decomposing Concealment Reveals What Makes It Depleting," *Journal of Experimental Psychology: General*, 143 (2014), 721–735.

NOTES

60. "Zuckerberg Senate Transcript 2018," Wikisource, https://en.wikisource.org/wiki/Zuckerberg_Senate_Transcript_2018.

61. Osmo Wiio, "How All Human Communication Fails, Except by Accident, or a Commentary of Wiio's Laws," trans. Jukka Korpela, (2010) http://jkorpela.fi/wiio.html.

62. Charles Krauthammer, "Kasparov: Deep Blue Funk," *Time*, February 26, 1996.

63. Sean Müller, Fleur van Rens, et al., "Embedding of Psycho-Perceptual-Motor Skills Can Improve Athlete Assessment and Training Programs," *Journal of Expertise* 2, no. 1 (March 2019) 14–22, https://www.journalofexpertise.org/articles/volume2_issue1/JoE_2019_2_1_M%C3%BCller.pdf.

64. SE, 31–46.

65. Rory Arnold, "How Artists and Architects See Things Differently Than Others," Earth.com News, June 28, 2017, https://www.earth.com/news/artists-architects-see-differently.

66. "Aussie Groth Hits Speedy Serves," Association of Tennis Professionals, May 13, 2012, https://www.atptour.com/en/news/groth-fast-serve.

67. Guardian Sport, "Returning a Pro Tennis Serve: Just Don't Watch the Ball," YouTube, July 13, 2018, youtube.com/watch?v=-8sBD5Wg2jQ&t=142s.

68. William Chase and Herbert Simon, "Skill in Chess: Experiments with Chess-Playing Tasks and Computer Simulation of Skilled Performance Throw Light on Some Human Perceptual and Memory Processes," American Scientist (1973): 394–403.

69. SE, 31–46.

70. Yu-Hsuan Chang and David Lane, "It Takes More Than Practice and Experience to Become a Chess Master: Evidence from a Child Prodigy and Adult Chess Players," *Journal Expertise*, 1 (2018).

71. CHB, 597.

72. William Chase and Herbert Simon, "Perception in Chess," *Cognitive Psychology* (1973): 55–81.

73. PEAK, 58.

74. Lee Green, *Sportswit* (Harper & Row, 1984) 169.

75. Charles Darwin, *The Descent of Man*, vol. 1, p. 3.

76. "Remarks by the President on the Affordable Care Act," Obama White House Archives, October 21, 2013, https://obamawhitehouse.archives.gov/the-press-office/2013/10/21/remarks-president-affordable-care-act.

77. David Fleming, "No More Questions," ESPN, October 4, 2016, https://www.espn.com/espn/feature/story/_/id/17703210/new-england-patriots-coach-bill-belichick-greatest-enigma-sports.

78. Steve Politi, "Bill Belichick's Masterful Super Bowl Game Plan Proves He Can Win Without Tom Brady," NJ.com, February 4, 2019, https://www.nj.com/giants/2019/02/bill-belichicks-masterful-super-bowl-game-plan-proves-he-can-win-without-tom-brady-politi.html; Jeff McLane, "In Bill Belichick's Greatest Achievement, Patriots Stuff Rams in Super Bowl LIII," *The Philadelphia Inquirer*, February 3, 2019, https://www.inquirer.com/eagles/super-bowl-game-score-patriots-rams-bill-belichick-tom-brady-sean-mcvay-jared-goff-20190204.html.

79. Dejan Kalinic, "Super Bowl 53: Patriots Played Like 'Champions,' Bill Belichick Says," *Sporting News*, February 3, 2019, https://www.sportingnews.com/us/nfl/news/new-england-patriots-la-rams-super-bowl-liii-bill-belichick/shgo9vdaxmjn1gb4fk831fi3p.

80. "Super Bowl LV Trophy Presentation and MVP Speech," NFL video, 5:32, February 7, 2021, https://www.youtube.com/watch?v=PXx7iF3hVCw.

81. Maegan Vasquez, "How Dr. Anthony Fauci Became Trump's Coronavirus Truth Teller," CNN, March 14, 2020, https://www.cnn.com/2020/03/14/politics/anthony-fauci-trump-coronavirus/index.html.

82. Michael Specter, "How Anthony Fauci Became America's Doctor," *The New Yorker*, April 10, 2020, https://www.newyorker.com/magazine/2020/04/20/how-anthony-fauci-became-americas-doctor.

83. James Freeman, "The Limits of Anthony Fauci's Expertise," *The Wall Street Journal*, May 13, 2020, https://www.wsj.com/articles/the-limits-of-anthony-faucis-expertise-11589392347.

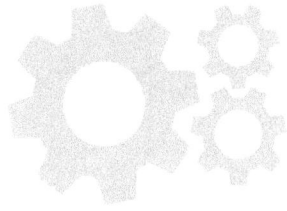

INDEX

Index

Temperance, 189
Tennis, 174, 199–200
"10,000-hour rule," 23, 90
Testing, 165
Thank you, saying, 140
Thin slicing, 68
Tombough, Clyde, 12
Trade associations, 56
Training, influence on expertise, 90
Trump, Donald, 41
Trust, 240
  as an emotion, 118
  building relationships and, 121–122
  carelessness with valuable assets and,
   153–154
  confidence and, 28
  in doctors, 32
  early evidence of experts possessing, 114
  foundation of, 111
  genetics and the ability to, 125–126
  imbalances and asymmetry of, 123–124
  importance of SMEs establishing, 240
  in one's motives, 115, 119–120
  in one's skills, 115, 116–117
  in people with confidence, 28
  in physicians, 32
  professional membership/certifications
   and, 55–56
  in sale transactions, 112–113
  SMEs establishing, 9–10, 240
  types of, 115
  violating, by throwing people under the
   bus, 166–167
Truth
  as less influential, 49–50
  sensitivity *versus*, 51–52
  SMEs needing more than, 50
  wrongness and, 59–60

U

Uber, 62
Under-delivering, 117

Unexpected events, being prepared for,
  212–213
United States Air Force Office of Scientific
  Research, 73
Unskilled, patience with the, 207–208

V

Valuable assets, protecting security of,
  153–154
Vision. *See also* Mutual vision, determining
  of experts, 173–174
  SME changing a customer's, 175–176
  three components of, 174
Vocabulary
  curse of knowledge and, 35
  metaphors, 186
  use of jargon, 155–156
Von Braun, Wernher, 165

W

Wambach, Abby, 195
Wattie, Nick, 90
Weaknesses, of competitors, 99, 101
Websites, 225, 233
Wheeler, McArthur, 207
White House Coronavirus Task Force, 239
Wiio, Osmo, 163
WikiLeaks, 149
Winfrey, Oprah, 23
Wrong, dealing with being, 59–61

Y

"Yes" answer, 159–161

Z

Zuckerberg, Mark, 157–158

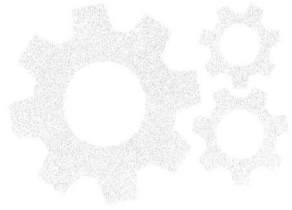

ABOUT THE AUTHOR

ALAN BERREY is the founder of Expert Dig, Inc., a research and training venture that is committed to the advancement of corporate experts. He has worked as a subject matter expert for decades, serving as the CEO of multiple start-up companies and as the vice president of business development at multiple technology companies. His corporate positions also include software product manager, project manager, department manager, and engineer.

He has served clients in dozens of industries including high-tech, manufacturing, financial services, telecommunications, transportation, health care, and government. Alan served as a communications specialist in the US Army Airborne Rangers. He holds a BS in computer science from Brigham Young University and an MBA from Carnegie Mellon University. He is the father of four and lives with his wife in Massachusetts.

Expert Dig

If you are interested in unlocking the immense potential of subject matter experts, please contact us at Expert Dig. We help subject matter experts, including sales consultants, solution engineers, customer success managers, and other technical professionals master their craft. We help bring expertise out of obscurity and maximize the expert's impact with clients, customers, colleagues, and partners. Our courses, training, and lectures are tailored to help experts become compelling agents of change.

www.ExpertDig.com